ASIA LIGHT

Ghillie James was food editor of 'Sainsbury's Magazine' for five years and now writes freelance from her home in Singapore for a number of magazines and newspapers such as 'BBC Good Food' and the 'Boston Globe'. She is also the author of health-conscious global cookbook 'Amazing Grains', which is full of nutritious recipes that reflect her love of eating healthy food, as well as 'Fresh from the Freezer' and 'Jams, Jelly & Relish'.

ASIA LIGHT

Healthy and Contemporary Asian Recipes

Ghillie James

Photography by Alicia Taylor
Kyle Books

Dedicated to our beautiful, smiling, forever bouncing baby boy, George

First published in Great Britain in 2015 by
Kyle Books, an imprint of Kyle Cathie Ltd
192–198 Vauxhall Bridge Road
London SW1V 1DX
general.enquiries@kylebooks.com
www.kylebooks.com

10 9 8 7 6 5 4 3 2 1

978 0 85783 277 1

Text © 2015 Ghillie James
Design © 2015 Kyle Books
Photography © 2015 Alicia Taylor

Designer: Aileen Lord
Photographer: Alicia Taylor
Food Stylist: Deborah Kaloper
Home Economist: Emma Christian
Nutritional Analysis: Fiona Hunter
Project Editor: Sophie Allen
Editorial Assistant: Hannah Coughlin
Production: Nic Jones, Gemma John and Lisa Pinnell

A Cataloguing in Publication record for this title is available from the British Library.

Colour reproduction by ALTA London.
Printed in China by Toppan Leefung Printing Ltd.

Thank-you to Shiva Designs shivadesignsbespoke.com, Korla korlahome.com and Spin Singapore spin-singapore.com (Spin items were used on pp. 15 – small and large bowl, 96, 141 - light blue cup).

All nutritional information excludes serving suggestions. The oven temperatures for ºC are for non-fan-assisted ovens, so turn down by 20ºC if you have a fan oven.

 (V) Vegetarian (VE) Vegan (L-GI) Low-GI (GF) Gluten-free (DF) Dairy-free

 (LS) Low sugar (LF) Low Fat

Contents

Introduction

Most people in Asia still cook food from scratch – using recipes handed down through generations and a dazzling array of the freshest produce. So why am I writing a book about making Asian food healthier? It's us Westerners, with our fondness for processed foods, whose diets contain way too much fat, sugar, salt, and preservatives, isn't it? Although Asian stir-fries, salads, curries and noodles contain loads of vitamins and minerals (which is why we should be eating them), many also contain too high quantities of salt, sugar and preservatives (often found in the jarred sauces and bottles used) and are deep-fried in oil. And so these Asian recipes can be equally dangerous when it comes to keeping a healthy heart or preventing diabetes.

Fiona Hunter, the nutritionist and food writer, says that, 'From a nutritional point of view the typical Asian diet has positives and negatives. On the plus side, it contains plenty of fruit and vegetables – much more than the typical Western diet – and a good selection of vegetables to boot, particularly leafy greens, which are all highly nutritious. Ingredients like shellfish, chicken and tofu are all good-quality, lean proteins so that's another plus point, with tofu providing phytochemicals, which are believed to help lower cholesterol. On the downside, Asian diets are typically very high in salt, calories and refined sugars, and it can also be high in saturated fat. Another problem is that when food is repeatedly deep-fried in any type of oil, some unsaturated fats are changed into trans-fats which are thought to be even worse for the heart than saturated fat. High intakes of salt are known to increase the risk of high blood pressure, which in turn increases the risk of heart disease and stroke. A high intake of saturated fat also increases the risk of heart disease and stroke because it pushes up blood cholesterol, which then starts to clogs blood vessels that take blood to the heart and brain.'

The good news is that making your favourite Asian dishes healthy is relatively easy to do if you make your own sauces, choose cuts of meat carefully – avoiding the fatty ones – and oven bake, stir-fry or grill rather than deep-fry. The inspiration for my recipes comes from Singapore, where I live, which is the most incredible melting pot of influences: from Chinese to Indian to Arab to Malay, only a skip and a hop away from Thailand, to Burma, Cambodia, Laos, Vietnam, Philippines, Malaysia, Brunei, East Timor, Indonesia, Japan and Korea. Singaporeans are obsessed with food and as a result the country is chock full of incredible eateries! What I love about it is that, although it is one of the richest countries in the world for its size, a rich Singaporean businessman is just as likely to be found eating his breakfast sitting on a stall outside a hawker centre as he is to be found in one of Asia's best high-end restaurants with award-winning chefs. There are also a great variety of places to shop, from the wet market selling bright and shiny fresh fish and colourful fruit and veg, just at the end of my road, to the health food shops and the many swanky shopping malls selling imported produce in the city centre.

In this book I will show you how simply swapping a jar of sauce for a combination of three to four storecupboard basics (I promise you don't need a cupboard full of weird bottles you will only use once!), will transform a once high salt and sugar stir-fry into a super healthy one. I've tweaked favourite curry recipes with quick to prepare homemade pastes (all freezeable for later) and lower fat coconut milk – reducing the additives and lowering the fat

content considerably. I also use leaner cuts of meat to speed the cooking up and to lower the fat. Plus, I remove all additional refined sugar from everything to show you how puddings, dressings and sauces needn't be bad for you. Favourite carb-filled recipes such as stir-fried white rice and sides using egg noodles have also been swapped for nutritious alternatives such as soba noodle salads and healthier steam-fried brown rice.

I do think that we should all be paying far more attention to what we are eating – stripping back our diets, having a look at what is in our cupboards and understanding what we, and our children, are cooking with and being fed. In a way, we should be starting from scratch again. We should all be eating as much home-grown fruit and veg, local meat, fresh fish, raw honey and whole grains as possible, plus the right quantity of the right fats. Really checking the amount of fat, sugar and salt in our diet is imperative – not just having a vague clue but monitoring what goes into the foods we are eating. Because we are undeniably what we eat. There is a growing body of evidence, which we simply can't ignore, that highlights the foods that can both cause or cure a whole host of illnesses. Too many of my young friends are afflicted by illnesses that I would, until recently, have associated with much older folk. And this upsurge is partly due to what we are now allowing ourselves to eat (as well, of course, as the stress involved with 21st century living).

So, what to do? Well, as far as sugar goes I'm not going to stick to the give it all up approach. I see why some people have to omit sugar from their diet because of their health. However, providing consumption is carefully monitored, I don't feel the need to be completely drastic – and I don't really like the idea of never eating honey or a fresh mango again because they

contain sugar (I also won't deny my children the occasional treat from the sweet shop or scoop of ice cream). But there is, without question, a worldwide necessity to reduce the amount of sugar being consumed and that change has to start in our own homes. We need to retrain our bodies to need less sugar. Sheila Dillon reported on Radio 4 *The Food Programme* that in the 18th century people were eating less than 4lb (1.8kg) sugar a year. By the 20th century it had shot up to as much as 80lb (36kg)! We are, according to some, eating toxic quantities of sugar. So we do need to cut back our sugar intake as much as possible, and if you've ever given up sugar in your tea or coffee, you will know that it takes time but your taste buds do adapt. Our children won't then have such crazy sweet cravings and the 'highs' that result from consuming sugar, the rise in Type 2 Diabetes will hopefully stop and we won't continue on the road to obesity. Personally, I now look at all food labels, especially at where sugar is on the list of ingredients (if it's near the start of the list then you can pretty much guarantee it's going to have too much). I try to limit my use of refined sugar where possible. I use honey as a first go to for a little sweetness in things and try to find raw as it contains all the goodness that honey should have. Stevia would be my next sugar replacement of choice (if I don't want the flavour of honey), followed by palm sugar.

The same applies to salt – we need to cut back, look closely at labels and when we do use it (and a lot of recipes do need a bit of salt to taste good) choose the right salt. Forget cheap and nasty table salt – which is highly processed. Try to use sea salt such as Malden or the 'pink' salt as it contains a whole load less nasties and has a higher mineral content. Buy sauces that are reduced in salt, such as soy, where possible. I guess when I say buy 'good quality' it tends to

mean the most expensive – but if that means less additives and preservatives then it is worth paying the extra. Kikkoman and Lee Kum Kee are two brands of Asian sauces that I trust. Our taste for salt is what nutritionists call a 'learnt response', which means that while we are born with a liking for sweet foods we learn to like salty foods. Unfortunately, it seems the more we eat the more we learn to like it and the less sensitive our taste buds become to it, but you can teach yourself to enjoy foods with less salt; it taks about 4 weeks to retrain your taste buds to enjoy the true flavour of food, not the salt.

Fat is a bit of a minefield, but choose leaner cuts of meat and don't add lard or pork fat, as you so often find in traditional Asian recipes, such as Char Kway teow noodles. I love coconut oil for its numerous health benefits and high smoke point. I have tried to use as little oil as possible while the research continues about which oils are good or bad for us.

With all of the above in mind, what I have found so interesting when developing recipes for this book is that taking classic Asian favourites and giving them a makeover to make them healthy hasn't made a jot of difference to their taste. It's improved them if anything! Some sensible, and mainly un-noticable, changes to the foods we love will make a huge difference. I have never liked or promoted the idea of eradicating major food groups in any diet, or indeed been on a 'diet', but this book shows you how eating a sensible balance of everything, and where possible removing 'processed' and 'refined' as much as you can, makes a great difference to how healthy your diet really is.

I hope you will enjoy this book, whether you are Asian, live in Asia, have been cooking Asian for years or a novice. All recipes are relatively easy and perfect for any occasion.

Starters & Nibbles

Though there's a time and place for sitting down at the table and eating a starter, by far my favourite way to eat a first course is to munch on a shared platter of goodies whilst sitting around having drinks and chatting. Asian starters are so wonderfully varied and often have interesting dips and sauces to dive into – perfect for sharing. Prawn & Lemongrass Pops, Indonesian Satay Skewers and Japanese Tsukene Chicken & Shiitake Meatballs can all be prepared way ahead of time, multiplied for larger parties, and quickly cooked and served on a large tray for guests to help themselves. And there's no need for garnishes or cutlery either, as the recipes are pretty enough and everything is designed to be eaten with fingers.

Although popular Asian starters such as crispy spring rolls and Thai fishcakes are undeniably delicious, they are not exactly the healthiest, and can often leave you feeling heavy and full before you've even sat down to dinner. This chapter provides plenty of alternative Asian nibbles that are a bit lighter and better for you. Not too far off-piste, but baked, grilled or barbecued rather than deep-fried and avoiding the high salt and sugar contained in many of the ready-made dipping sauces. And for super-easy options, try the Spicy Asian Nuts or Healthy-style Crispy Seaweed instead of nuts or crisps.

SPICY ASIAN NUTS

These are super moreish and pretty healthy too. Although they do have a bit of added salt which is essential to the flavour (use pink if you can as it has better flavour), they don't have any added butter or oil, which so many recipes for roasted nuts do. There's enough for a cereal bowl full – a good amount for 6–8 people to nibble on with a cold beer.

Makes about 180g nuts

(V) (LG) (GF) (DF) (LS)

Per 20g nuts 127 cals | 11g fat | 2g sat fat
5g protein | 3g carbs | 1.5g sugar | trace salt

175g unroasted nuts, such as peanuts, pistachios, almonds and cashews
½ teaspoon five spice powder
3 good pinches of cayenne pepper
¼ teaspoon ground ginger
1 teaspoon pink or white sea salt flakes
1 heaped tablespoon pumpkin seeds
1 teaspoon sesame seeds
¾ teaspoon clear honey, preferably raw

Preheat the oven to 200°C/gas mark 6. Line a baking tray with baking parchment.

Scatter the nuts onto the prepared tray and bake for about 5 minutes. Meanwhile, mix the spices with the salt. Scatter the pumpkin and sesame seeds in with the nuts, then sprinkle with the spice mix. Toss to coat all over. Return the nuts and seeds to the oven for 3–5 minutes, or until they are brown but not dark, then remove and drizzle with the honey before tossing again to completely coat. Leave to cool, break up gently using your fingers and store in a jar for up to 2 weeks.

HEALTHY-STYLE CRISPY SEAWEED

All hail the kale, for all its wonderful superfood powers! You will find yourself munching on this 'seaweed' all day long as it's totally addictive, and what's more, you don't need to feel guilty eating it. Charlotte, my assistant, is a super-healthy eater and this recipe is her guilt-free snack of choice. The key is in the preparation – if the kale is at all damp or not well spread out on the baking tray, it will go chewy rather than crispy. Traditional Chinese seaweed includes a lot more oil and sugar, but this is an even better version – and much healthier! Pink sea salt contains more minerals than white sea salt, so choose this if you can. Don't use palm sugar crystals – it's a block of palm sugar you need. If you can't find this use dark brown soft sugar instead.

Serves 4

(V) (VE) (LG) (GF) (DF) (LS) (LF)

Per serving: 45 cals | 4g fat↓ 3g sat fat
2g protein | 1g carbs | 1g sugar | 1.3g salt

300g fresh kale, stems removed (trimmed weight about 200g)
3 teaspoons coconut or light olive oil
1 teaspoon pink or white sea salt flakes
½ teaspoon grated palm sugar or dark brown soft sugar

Preheat the oven to 160°C fan or 180°C/gas mark 4 (it's preferable to use the fan setting on the oven). Line 2 baking trays with baking parchment.

Cut the kale leaves into large pieces (approximately 7–8cm in diameter). Wash the kale and then dry it thoroughly (ideally use a salad spinner) and then pat it completely dry with kitchen paper.

Spread the kale leaves on the lined trays in a single layer. Drizzle with the oil and sprinkle with the salt flakes. Thoroughly toss the kale, so it is well coated with the oil and salt, and spread it out again.

Cook in the oven for about 10 minutes, keeping a close eye on it to make sure it doesn't burn at all – the kale should stay green and not brown at all or it will taste bitter.

Remove from the oven and sprinkle over the sugar. Toss the kale well, then spread it out evenly and return to the oven for 3 minutes. Remove from the oven and leave for 3 minutes to crisp up and then toss and serve immediately.

SIMPLE ASIAN MUSSELS & CLAMS

A bowl of fresh steaming mussels in broth is hard to beat for a starter or lunch. Rather than the usual French moules marinière, we often cook ours in a fragrant combo of lemongrass, garlic, ginger and coriander. Personally, I'm not a fan of adding cream or coconut milk, as I like the pure taste of the aromatics with the mussel and clam juices, but you can add a splash of either if you like. Just don't forget the requisite bread for dunking!

Serves 4-6

PER SERVING (FOR 6): 80 cals | 2g fat
0.5g sat fat | 10g protein | 4g carbs
1.5g sugar | 0.6g salt

1 teaspoon light olive oil
2 garlic cloves, thinly sliced
5cm piece of fresh ginger, peeled and finely chopped or grated
1 lemongrass stalk, tough outer leaves removed and remaining inner stalk very finely chopped
2 fresh kaffir lime leaves (or 3-4 dried), shredded (optional)
1 long red chilli, deseeded and finely chopped
500g live mussels, scrubbed, rinsed and beards removed (discard any that stay open when sharply tapped)
500g live clams, scrubbed, rinsed and beards removed (discard any that stay open when sharply tapped)
bunch of spring onions, trimmed and cut into 2-3cm lengths
5 tablespoons white wine or sake
juice of 1 lime
2-3 tablespoons chopped coriander
salt and freshly ground black pepper
crusty bread, to serve

In a very large saucepan heat the oil, add the garlic, ginger, lemongrass, lime leaves (if using) and chilli and gently sauté for 3-4 minutes before adding the shellfish, spring onions and wine or sake, along with 2 tablespoons of cold water. Put a lid on the pan, turn up the heat and cook for about 5 minutes, shaking every so often.

Remove the lid and discard any mussels or clams that have not opened. Add the lime juice and coriander, stir, then taste and adjust the seasoning. Divide between bowls with all the juices poured over. Serve with crusty bread.

STARTERS

PRAWN & LEMONGRASS POPS

Not dissimilar to the Thai fishcakes we all know and love, but with handy lemongrass stalk handles. They are a wonderful treat for guests when they come out of the kitchen looking so pretty and smelling wonderful. The good news is that they are super healthy too! Simple to make, you can prepare the sauce and the pops a few hours ahead of time. Then just cook them in a non-stick pan and keep them warm just before your guests arrive. If using the recipe for Thai paste in this book, then add 3 teaspoons, but you might find less is sufficient if using a shop-bought brand, which can be stronger. If you want a simpler recipe, you can just make them into patties instead of skewering.

Makes 14–16 pops

PER POP (FOR 16): 41 cals | 1g fat 0.1g sat fat | 7g protein | 2g carbs 1.5g sugar | 0.5g salt

750g raw prawns, peeled and deveined (peeled weight about 375g)
200g skinless, boneless white fish fillet
3 tablespoons chopped coriander leaves and stems
2 fresh or 3–4 dried kaffir lime leaves, very finely shredded (optional)
2–3 teaspoons Thai Red Curry Paste (see page 174), depending on the strength used
2 teaspoons fish sauce
1½ teaspoons sweet chilli sauce or ½ red chilli and 1 teaspoon clear honey, preferably raw
1½ teaspoons cornflour
zest of 1 unwaxed lime
6 lemongrass stalks (for the handles), tough outer leaves discarded, and each stem cut into 3
2 teaspoons coconut or light olive oil, or spray oil

For the nuoc cham dipping sauce
1 garlic clove
1 large red chilli, roughly chopped (deseed for less heat)
juice of 1 lime
1 tablespoon fish sauce
1½ tablespoons rice vinegar
2½ teaspoons clear honey or a sprinkling of stevia powder, to taste

Roughly chop the prawns and fish, then pat dry with kitchen paper. Place in a food processor with the coriander, lime leaves (if using), curry paste, fish and chilli sauces, cornflour and lime zest. Carefully pulse until the mixture is finely chopped but not so much that it has turned to a paste. Transfer to a bowl, cover and chill for 20 minutes.

Meanwhile, for the sauce, using a pestle and mortar, pound the garlic and chilli together until crushed. Transfer to a small bowl and add the remaining sauce ingredients plus 2 tablespoons of cold water, and stir well to combine.

With damp hands, shape the fish mixture into 14–16 equal-sized balls and mould onto the lemongrass sticks to form round, but slightly flattened 'lollipops'. Transfer to an oiled plate, then chill, uncovered, for at least 1 hour or until you're ready to cook.

Brush or spray the pops with the oil and fry in a non-stick frying pan or cook over a medium heat on a griddle or barbecue for 6–8 minutes, carefully turning, until they are cooked through. Serve with the dipping sauce.

ZESTY, SPICY BARBECUED SQUID WITH MANGO

Kiwi has a great tenderising effect on squid, so is a wonderful addition to the marinade. I like to cook these on the barbecue. Serve the mini skewers as canapés or choose the long skewers and serve with salad as a starter. They can also be grilled or griddled.

Makes 12–14 mini skewers or 6 long skewers

PER MINI SKEWER (FOR 14): 63 cals
2.5g fat | 0.5g sat fat | 7g protein | 3g carbs
2.5g sugar | 0.3g salt

For the marinade
1 ripe kiwi fruit, unpeeled and thinly sliced
1 teaspoon sweet chilli sauce
1 teaspoon coconut or light olive oil, plus extra for brushing
1 teaspoon fish sauce
1 teaspoon reduced-salt soy sauce
pinch of dried chilli flakes
1 heaped teaspoon finely grated fresh ginger

For the skewers
600g fresh squid
1 medium-sized ripe mango, peeled and cut into chunks
2 tablespoons finely chopped coriander leaves
2 tablespoons lime juice (about 1 lime)
1 ½ tablespoons coconut or light olive oil

Soak 12–14 mini or 6 long wooden skewers in cold water (this prevents them from burning during cooking).

Combine the marinade ingredients in a non-metallic bowl and stir well.

To prepare the squid, remove the purple fine skin from the outside, then remove the head and tentacles with a knife. Slice the squid down the inside to open out and remove anything inside – there will probably be a plastic-like strip and a bit of slime. Wash the squid thoroughly under cold running water. Cut the squid into 3 x 6cm pieces and score it (I use the tentacles too, but that's up to you).

Add the squid strips to the marinade and toss to coat. Cover and set aside to marinate in the fridge for 30 minutes to 1 hour.

Thread alternate pieces of squid and mango onto the soaked skewers. Preheat the barbecue to high and brush or spray the grill rack with oil. Cook the skewers for about 1 minute on each side, letting the edges char slightly. Transfer to a warm plate. Mix the coriander with the lime juice and oil and drizzle it over the kebabs to serve.

CRISPY BAKED CRAB CAKES

I prefer to serve finger food starters to enjoy with a long cool drink outside. It's less formal than a plated starter and means that everyone can relax a little longer before sitting at the table. Baking the crab cakes is not only healthier but also prevents your house from smelling like a fish shop just before guests arrive!

Crab is low in calories as well as being high in vitamins and minerals. You can use canned crab if finding the fresh meat is tricky – not quite as good but still delicious.

I like to serve the cakes with Nuoc Cham Sauce for dipping. Alternatively, whizz avocado with some lime juice, seasoning and a blob of wasabi and spoon a dollop on top of each cake before serving.

Makes 12 bite-sized cakes

PER CAKE: 64 cals | 2.5g fat | 0.7g sat fat
4.5g protein | 6.5g carbs | 0.5g sugar
0.4g salt

Tip: To freeze the cakes, bake as per the recipe and set aside to cool. Transfer to an airtight lidded container and freeze. To reheat, bake from frozen for 15–20 minutes or until piping hot at 200°C/gas mark 6.

For the bouillon (if using fresh crab)
1 tablespoon sea salt
6 peppercorns
½ onion, roughly chopped
2 bay leaves
1 large garlic clove, crushed
100ml white wine
1 lemon, sliced

150g fresh white crabmeat or 1 live crab, about 500g
2 spring onions, finely chopped, green ends reserved for garnish
1 teaspoon grated fresh ginger
2 teaspoons reduced-salt soy sauce
2 tablespoons low-fat mayonnaise
1 garlic clove, crushed
9 heaped tablespoons panko breadcrumbs
1 free-range egg white, lightly beaten
zest of ½ unwaxed lime
1 tablespoon lime juice
2 pinches of cayenne pepper
½ teaspoon sesame seeds (optional)
2 teaspoons coconut or light olive oil, plus spray oil
Nuoc Cham Dipping Sauce (see page 19) or sweet chilli sauce, to serve

Line a baking tray with baking parchment and spray it with oil.

To cook a live crab, put 1.5 litres of cold water in a pan just wide enough to fit the crab. Add the bouillon ingredients and bring slowly to the boil. Simmer for 15 minutes, then bring back up to the boil. Add the crab and cook for 6 minutes (12 minutes per 1kg), turn off the heat and leave in the water to cool completely. Take the crab apart and remove the white meat.

Combine the crabmeat, spring onions, ginger, soy sauce, mayonnaise, garlic, 4 tablespoons of the bread crumbs, egg white, lime zest and juice and cayenne. Stir well to combine, then cover and chill for 1 hour.

In a shallow dish, mix the remaining bread crumbs with the sesame seeds (if using) and the oil. Form into 12 cakes and roll in the crumbs to coat. Place on the lined baking tray and chill until ready to use.

Preheat the oven to 220°C/gas mark 7. Spray the cakes all over with oil. Bake for 15 minutes or until golden. Garnish with the spring onion ends and serve with Nuoc Cham Dipping Sauce or sweet chilli sauce.

SALMON OR TUNA WASABI TARTARE

Though I love the idea of salmon or tuna tartare as a starter, I do find it incredibly filling. So, I prefer to serve it as a pre-dinner eat to have with drinks – a beautiful bowlful for guests to scoop out at their leisure and pile onto crisp toasted croûtes or baguette. It also goes beautifully with a cocktail such as the Lime Mint Vodka Cooler on page 166.

This Japanese-inspired tartare is super healthy as it is packed with nutrients and natural fish oils from the raw fish, plus citrus juice and fresh herbs. It also has a hint of wasabi, but it's not too overwhelming and works well with salmon or tuna. Adding avocado is a rather nice nutritious extra, if you fancy it. And if you want to be carb-free, serve with endive or crispy gem lettuce leaves to pile the tartare into.

You can make this up to 2 hours ahead, but add the lime and herbs at the last minute or the herbs will lose their colour and the juice will start to 'cook' the fish.

Serves 3–4 as a starter or 8 as a canapé

(LGI) (DF) (LS) (LF)

Per canapé (including avocado): 142 cals 6.5g fat 1g sat fat | 10g protein | 11g carbs 0.8g sugar | 0.4g salt

300g very fresh, good-quality salmon or tuna, preferably sashimi grade, finely chopped into 6–8mm dice
1 tablespoon finely chopped spring onion
2 teaspoons grated ginger
zest of 1 unwaxed lime
1–2 teaspoons wasabi paste or ½ green chilli, very finely chopped
1 tablespoon snipped chives
1 tablespoon chopped coriander (optional)
1 tablespoon chopped Thai basil
½ avocado, finely chopped (optional)
juice of 1 ½ limes
sea salt and freshly ground black pepper
toasted thinly sliced baguette, croûtes or Melba toast, to serve
olive oil and halved chives, if serving as a starter

Place the fish in a bowl with the spring onion, ginger, lime zest and wasabi or chilli and a good grinding of black pepper. Mix together, cover and chill in the fridge.

Around 10 minutes before serving, stir in the herbs, avocado (if using), and most of the lime juice, plus a sprinkling of sea salt. Stir well and add extra wasabi, chilli, lime juice or salt, to taste.

Serve as a canapé with toasted baguette, croûtes or Melba toast. Or to serve as a starter, oil 4 small ramekins and divide the tartare between them. Turn out onto plates and serve with a drizzle of oil, a couple of halved chives rested on the top and the crisp bread on the side.

Tip: Putting the fish in the freezer for an hour or so is a good way to firm it up before attempting to cut it into fine dice using a very sharp knife, but whatever happens don't be tempted to whizz it up.

STARTERS

TUNA SASHIMI

Lexy is a new friend in Singapore, and it was quickly apparent at our first meeting that she is a great food fanatic and indeed a great cook! This is an adaptation of her fail-safe starter, which can easily be made in advance.

I'm not trying to make it sound more complicated by giving the size of tuna used, as it doesn't matter too much, but for those who are sticklers for detail it may be handy to visualise it!

Serves 6-8 as a starter or 10-12 as a canapé

Per serving (for 12): 50 cals | 2g fat 0.5g sat fat | 5.5g protein | 2.5g carbs 2g sugar | 0.4g salt

Tip: For canapés, serve on spoons or in baby lettuce leaves. Simply place a slice of tuna on the spoon or lettuce leaf and top with a little piece of pickled ginger, the salad (chop the apple even finer to fit) and a drizzle of dressing.

2 rectangular blocks of tuna loin, each about 250-300g in weight and 13–15cm long x 5–8cm wide x 2–3cm thick, patted dry with kitchen paper
2 teaspoons coconut or light olive oil
1 teaspoon wasabi paste
2 teaspoons black sesame seeds
2 teaspoons white sesame seeds
1 green apple, peeled, cored and cut into fine matchsticks
½ English cucumber or ¾ Japanese cucumber, about 150g, deseeded and cut into fine matchsticks
2 spring onions, finely shredded
½ lime
2-3 tablespoons pickled ginger
sea salt and ground white pepper

For the dressing
1 ½ tablespoons tamari
1 tablespoon mirin
1 teaspoon sesame oil
½ teaspoon grated ginger
1 tablespoon lime juice
½ teaspoon clear honey, preferably raw

Mix 1 teaspoon of the oil with the wasabi and brush it all over the tuna. Season all over with a little salt and white pepper. Mix the black and white sesame seeds on a plate and roll the tuna in the seeds until coated.

Brush a non-stick frying pan with the remaining oil, then heat until very hot but not smoking hot. Add the tuna to the pan and quickly sear each side of the loins, keeping them moving every 5–10 seconds or so in the pan so the tuna seals evenly – it should turn from pink to pale brown but it needs to remain completely raw in the middle and the sesame seeds shouldn't burn at all. Remove to cool on a plate, then wrap in clingfilm and chill for 2 hours or until ready to serve.

Toss the apple with the cucumber, spring onions, a squeeze of lime and a pinch of sea salt, transfer to the fridge until ready to serve. Mix all the dressing ingredients together and keep in the fridge.

Arrange little piles of the apple salad on individual plates. Thinly slice the tuna, using a very sharp knife, and arrange next to the salad, along with a small mound of pickled ginger. Serve the dressing separately.

STEAMED WONTONS

Our favourite family lunch is to go to one of the many Din Tai Fung outlets in Singapore for a feast of Xiao Long Bao, steamed dumplings and wontons. We always devour everything, and the wonderful food, busy waiters and buzzing atmosphere make us feel very lucky to live in Asia.

Wontons are super easy to make at home. Whether you want a healthy broth with tasty simmered wontons, a platter of freshly steamed dumplings with some soy chilli sauce or the more naughty but delicious crispy wontons – this recipe covers them all. Buy the wrappers from a Chinese supermarket or online and keep them in the freezer. The filled wontons also freeze beautifully, if well covered and sealed, for a few weeks, so make a big batch, open, freeze and pull out a few as required. You can vary the fillings too – mushroom and water chestnut, simple prawn or a spicier version with chilli, for example.

Makes 58 wontons

PER WONTON WITH SAUCE: 17 cals | 1g fat
0.2g sat fat | 1.5g protein | 1g carbs
0.2g sugar | 0.15g salt

For the wontons
58 square wonton wrappers
butterhead or iceberg lettuce leaves, for steaming

For the stuffing
280g lean pork mince
120g raw peeled prawns (about 250g unpeeled), finely chopped
2 teaspoons reduced-salt soy sauce
2 tablespoons snipped chives
2 tablespoons chopped coriander leaves
4 water chestnuts, freshly peeled or canned, finely chopped
1 tablespoon grated fresh ginger
1 ½ tablespoons Shaoxing Chinese cooking wine or dry sherry
2 teaspoons sesame oil
1 tablespoon cornflour

For the dipping sauce
4 teaspoons reduced-salt soy sauce
3 teaspoons sesame oil
2 teaspoons sweet chilli sauce
1–2 tablespoons lime juice

Place all the stuffing ingredients in a large bowl and using your hands, mix well to bind. Chill for at least 1 hour or up to 24 hours. The filling can be frozen at this stage, if required.

Take a wrapper and, using a finger, brush a little cold water around two of the wonton square's edges (wet the two edges of the square that meet to a point rather than opposites). Place about ¾ teaspoon of the filling in the middle and fold over the dry edges to meet the wet ones, sealing firmly to make a triangle. Now wet the two longer points of the triangle and bring up to meet and seal in the middle – make a little twist if the dumplings are not sealing easily. Repeat to use all the wrappers and filling. Place the wontons in a single layer on a tray in the fridge, covered with clingfilm, or freeze.

Recipe continues overleaf...

STARTERS

For the sauce, mix together the soy sauce, sesame oil and sweet chilli sauce in a small bowl and add a little lime juice. Taste the sauce and add a little more of any of the ingredients, if necessary.

Heat a steamer and place 5-6 lettuce leaves in the base of the steamer basket. Place the wontons in the steamer, about 2-3 cm apart, and steam for 3-4 minutes until cooked. Repeat until all the wontons are cooked. Serve with the sauce for dipping.

For Crispy Wontons: Make the wontons as above. Heat 7.5cm of light olive oil in a small saucepan or wok, until a piece of bread gently bubbles and sizzles when added. Add 5-6 wontons to the oil and cook in batches for 3 minutes or so, turning them over in the oil, until deep golden. Drain thoroughly on kitchen paper and serve with the sauce as above.

PER WONTON: 33 cals | 2.5g fat | 0.5g sat fat | 1.5g protein | 1g carbs | 0.2g sugar | 0.1g salt

For Wonton Soup Serves 4: For this recipe you will need an Aromatic Chicken Broth (see page 132) as your base and 12 wontons (I usually make a big batch and freeze the remainder). I like to add mushrooms and pak choi to the soup but you can use any vegetables, as long as they cook quickly.

Heat 1 litre of Aromatic Chicken Broth. When it starts to boil, add 175g enoki mushrooms (alternatively use quartered button, some oyster or halved canned and drained straw mushrooms) and 200g trimmed, shredded pak choi. Then add 12 wontons and cook in the boiling stock for 3 minutes. Serve 3 wontons per bowl, covered with the stock and vegetables and garnished with chopped coriander leaves.

PER SERVING: 117 cals | 3.8g fat | 1g sat fat | 16g protein | 4g carbs | 1.5g sugar | 1g salt

JAPANESE TSUKENE CHICKEN & SHIITAKE MEATBALLS WITH ORANGE GLAZE

This recipe ticks the box for canapés, soups and main courses as these sweet-glazed super-delicious meatballs can be speared with a cocktail stick, added to a bowl of steaming broth and noodles or served with rice. I like to include water chestnuts – they're not strictly authentic, but then again neither is the lower salt and sugar orange glaze I've put them with – but it's just as tasty as less healthy options.

Chicken mince is a great lower-fat alternative to pork or beef mince and these meatballs are baked rather than fried – they've still got all the taste but less fat. I often make a larger amount, then open-freeze the uncooked meatballs on baking parchment, and throw them in a bag to pull out at a later date, defrost and bake as per the recipe. My children also love them cold in their packed lunch boxes or on a picnic.

Makes 40 meatballs

PER BALL: 34 cals | 0.7g fat | 1g sat fat
4g protein | 3g carbs | 1.8g sugar | 0.2g salt

spray oil
1 small onion, finely chopped
1 large garlic clove, chopped
6 shiitake mushrooms, finely chopped
1 carrot, grated
600g chicken mince
5 water chestnuts, finely chopped
2 heaped teaspoons grated fresh ginger
2 tablespoons snipped chives
2 heaped tablespoons cornflour
2 teaspoons toasted sesame seeds
2 teaspoons sesame oil
2 teaspoons tamari or reduced-salt soy sauce
freshly ground black pepper

For the glaze
4 tablespoons fresh orange juice
2 tablespoons clear honey, preferably raw
2 tablespoons tamari or reduced-salt soy sauce
4 tablespoons mirin
2 teaspoons toasted sesame seeds
few snipped spring onions or chives, to serve

Preheat the oven to 220°C/gas mark 7. Line a baking tray with baking parchment and spray it with oil.

Spray a non-stick saucepan with oil and add the onion. Cook over a gentle heat for a couple of minutes before adding the garlic, mushrooms and carrot. Stir-fry for a minute, then add a tablespoon or so of cold water and cook for a further 3 minutes or so.

Transfer the cooked vegetables to a bowl and cool before adding all the remaining meatball ingredients, plus a grinding of black pepper. Mix everything together with wet hands, form into 40 walnut-sized balls and transfer to the lined baking tray. Spray the tops of the balls with oil and bake for 10–12 minutes or until starting to brown on top.

Meanwhile, put all the glaze ingredients into a saucepan and simmer until it starts to turn syrupy. Brush the meatballs with the glaze, then turn over and brush the other sides. Return to the oven for 4–5 minutes. Sprinkle with a few snipped spring onions or chives and put any extra glaze in a bowl for dipping. Serve the meatballs with cocktail sticks.

INDONESIAN SATAY SKEWERS

Singapore is a satay mecca. Stall holders at Lau Pau Sat market can always be seen barbecuing these delicious sticks and their sauce for the passing locals and tourists – a combination of spicy marinated skewers of chicken, beef, lamb and sometimes squid or prawns served with a delicious peanut dipping sauce.

It's also a popular dish in Indonesia, Thailand and Malaysia, and I have eaten and enjoyed it in all three places. We often go out for satay at lunchtime and I couldn't be happier seeing my children eating this healthy option, chargrilled over coals, with the rice cubes it's traditionally served with and chunks of cucumber.

However, they are also a really simple starter or finger food as they can be completely prepared in advance and only need minimal cooking on the barbecue or under the grill. Although peanuts are high in calories, this sauce is made with the non-salted type and light coconut milk for a healthier option.

Makes 24 mini or 12 long skewers

(LGI) (DF) (LS)

PER MINI CHICKEN SKEWER: 62 cals | 3g fat 1g sat fat | 6.5g protein | 2g carbs | 1.5g sugar | 0.2g salt

1 heaped teaspoon coriander seeds
4cm piece of fresh ginger, peeled and roughly chopped
2 garlic cloves, roughly chopped
2 fresh (or 3 dried) kaffir lime leaves, chopped
2 teaspoons reduced-salt soy sauce
2 teaspoons coconut or light olive oil
1 teaspoon ground turmeric
1 lemongrass stalk, tough outer leaves removed and remaining inner stalk very finely chopped
8 chicken thighs or 4 chicken breasts or 3 rib-eye steaks, cut into strips, or 36 large peeled raw prawns

For the sauce
spray oil
4cm piece of fresh ginger, peeled and grated
2 garlic cloves, chopped
½ onion, finely chopped
1 large red chilli, deseeded and finely chopped
100g unsalted roasted peanuts
100ml light coconut milk
3 teaspoons clear honey, preferably raw, or palm sugar
3 teaspoons reduced-salt soy sauce
juice of 1 ½ limes (about 2 ½ tablespoons)
2 tablespoons chopped fresh coriander
cucumber chunks, to serve

Place 24 mini or 12 long wooden skewers to soak in cold water (this prevents them from burning during cooking).

Heat a small, non-stick frying pan over a medium heat, add the coriander seeds, and shake the pan until they start to brown and give off a nutty aroma. Crush the toasted seeds using a pestle and mortar. Add the ginger, garlic cloves, lime leaves, soy sauce, oil, turmeric, lemongrass and 2 teaspoons of cold water and pound together until it forms a paste (if you like you can do this in a mini blender). Transfer to a large bowl and add the chicken, beef or prawns and toss well to coat. Marinate the chicken or beef for 30 minutes or more if you like, and the prawns for no more than 30 minutes.

To make the sauce, spray a non-stick pan with oil and add the ginger and garlic with the onion and chilli. Cook gently, stirring every so often, until soft. Meanwhile, pound the peanuts using a pestle and mortar or whizz them in a mini blender until they are not quite completely ground (it's good to have some texture). Add the nuts, coconut milk, honey and soy sauce along with 100ml of cold water to the pan and simmer gently for 5–10 minutes. Add the lime juice and coriander (reserve 1 teaspoon to garnish), then taste and add more soy sauce, honey or lime juice if required. Stir in a little extra water if the sauce is too thick.

Preheat the grill to high or heat a griddle pan or barbecue. Thread the marinated meat or prawns onto the skewers and cook for 4–8 minutes, depending on the meat used, or until cooked through. Garnish with the reserved coriander and serve with the satay sauce and cucumber.

FRESH DUCK, SPRING ONION & HOISIN ROLLS

Everyone loves crispy duck pancakes! The traditional way to eat them is with Chinese-style pancakes, slathered with sauce and a mound of not-so-healthy roasted duck. However, I like this healthier version, which although contains all the elements of the crispy duck pancakes we know and love, is made with rice paper wrappers, vermicelli, leaner duck meat, plenty of crunchy cucumber, lettuce and spring onion and a tasty dash of sauce.

If you like, you can skip the noodles and keep to the traditional way – just duck, shredded vegetables and hoisin. The noodles and lettuce make the rolls a bit healthier, give them some shape and are a good option if preparing them in advance. The rolls can be made ahead of time and served with drinks – they are great for guests to just pick up with their fingers and enjoy.

Makes 12 rolls

PER ROLL: 66 cals | 2.5g fat | 1g sat fat
6g protein | 4.5g carbs | 0.7g sugar
0.1g salt

40g rice vermicelli noodles
12 rice paper wrappers
3–4 teaspoons hoisin sauce, plus extra to serve
½ English cucumber, cut into matchsticks
4 spring onions, shredded
6 butterhead or garden lettuce leaves, 2 shredded and the rest left whole for covering the rolls in the fridge
250g cooked lean roast duck meat, shredded (see page 137)
1 teaspoon toasted sesame seeds

Put the noodles in a large bowl and pour over boiling water. Leave for 3–4 minutes until soft, then rinse under cold water and drain, then using scissors cut into manageable lengths. Place the filling ingredients in individual bowls to set up a production line.

Pour 3–5cm of cold water into a wide shallow bowl. Put a rice paper wrapper into the water and wait until it just starts to give a little. Transfer it onto a board and start to assemble your roll. Using the back of a spoon smear a small amount of hoisin sauce on the wrapper. Place some noodles and a couple of strips of cucumber along the bottom and then neatly, going horizontally across nearly the full length of the paper, top with spring onions, lettuce and duck. Finish with a sprinkling of sesame seeds. Fold over both ends and then roll up as tightly as you can, to make a neat package. Repeat to make the remaining rolls. If you need to make them in advance, place the rolls in containers, cover with some lettuce leaves to keep them moist – most other things will stick – and chill for up to 4 hours.

Cut each roll in half and arrange on a platter. Serve with a little extra hoisin on the side, if you like.

BEEF, SPRING ONION & ASPARAGUS NEGIMAKI

Serve these negimaki – traditional Japanese juicy spring onion and asparagus-stuffed beef rolls – either with sticks or napkins to wipe your fingers.

The beef needs to be cut across the grain into thin strips, so you'll need a super-sharp knife to do this. You can use sirloin steak instead of the fillet, but you'll need a thick piece with a small diameter. Photograph on page 33.

Makes 12 rolls

PER ROLL: 50 cals | 2g fat | 0.7g sat fat
5g protein | 3.5g carbs | 2.5g sugar
0.5g salt

For the marinade
2 teaspoons grated fresh ginger
2 garlic cloves, grated
1 ½ tablespoons clear honey, preferably raw
1 teaspoon sesame oil
2 tablespoons tamari or reduced-salt soy sauce
1 ½ tablespoons mirin

For the beef
1 x 250g thin, long piece of beef fillet, trimmed
12 spring onions, trimmed
6 thick or 12 fine asparagus spears, trimmed
1 teaspoon toasted sesame seeds

Mix all the marinade ingredients together in a large bowl. Slice the beef across the grain very thinly into approximately 12 rounds, 3mm or so thick. Place the beef slices in the marinade and set aside to marinate for between 20 minutes and 1 hour.

Remove the beef from the marinade with a slotted spoon and put onto a plate. Keep the marinade in the fridge until ready to cook the beef.

Bring a medium pan of salted water to the boil and blanch the spring onions and asparagus, depending on thickness, for 30–60 seconds (they need to retain their crunch but just lose their rawness). Drain and transfer to a bowl of iced water or chill under cold running water, drain again and pat dry with kitchen paper.

Cut each spring onion and asparagus spear in half (cut the thicker asparagus lengthways too) and put two pieces of spring onion and two bits of asparagus onto the end of a strip of beef. Roll each strip all the way along the vegetables, so that there is just a little poking out one end. Transfer to a non-stick baking tray spaced well apart. Keep in the fridge until 10 minutes before you are ready to cook.

Preheat the grill to high. Brush the beef rolls with some of the remaining marinade, then pop the baking tray as close to the grill as you can. Cook the rolls for 1–2 minutes, then carefully turn over, brush again with marinade and cook the other side. Serve immediately sprinkled with the toasted sesame seeds.

VIETNAMESE SUMMER ROLLS

Vietnamese-style fresh spring rolls are a great healthy option – they're packed with nutritious veg, herbs and noodles and dipped in a fat-free dressing. I think they look very pretty cut in half on the diagonal – and it also makes them a bit easier to pick up and eat. Meat, fish or veggie – the choice is yours, or make a combination to suit all tastes. Be adventurous too – avocado and sliced fresh mango are wonderful additions to any of the fillings. Photograph on page 33.

Makes 12 rolls

Per roll (pork filling): 88 cals | 4g fat
1g sat fat | 6g protein | 7g carbs
2.5g sugar | 0.4g salt

Per roll (prawn filling): 71 cals | 3g fat
0.5g sat fat | 5g protein | 5.5g carbs
2.5g sugar | 0.4g salt

40g rice vermicelli noodles
2 tablespoons chopped mint
1 tablespoon chopped Thai or sweet basil leaves
2 Chinese chives or 6–8 English chives, cut into 10cm lengths
2 tablespoons chopped coriander
¼ cucumber, deseeded and cut into thin matchsticks
1 large carrot, finely grated
6 butterhead or garden lettuce leaves, 2 shredded and the rest left whole for covering the rolls in the fridge
4 tablespoons salted, roasted peanuts, chopped
150g cooked, shredded lean roast pork, duck or chicken, or 12 cooked and peeled tiger prawns, halved lengthways
12 rice paper wrappers

For the dipping sauce
1 large red chilli, deseeded (optional) and chopped
1 garlic clove, peeled
juice of 1 lime
1 tablespoon fish sauce
1 ½ tablespoons rice vinegar
2 ½ teaspoons clear honey, preferably raw, or stevia powder, to taste

Put the noodles in a large bowl and pour over boiling water. Leave for 3–4 minutes until soft, then rinse under cold water and drain. Using scissors, cut into manageable lengths. Place all the herbs in one bowl and the remaining filling ingredients in individual bowls to set up a production line.

Pour 3–5cm of cold water into a wide shallow bowl. Put a rice paper wrapper into the water and wait until it just starts to give a little. Transfer it onto a board and place a couple of strips of cucumber along the bottom and then neatly, going horizontally across nearly the full length of the paper, top with a little of the carrot, noodles, herbs, lettuce, peanuts and some shredded meat or a couple of halved prawns. Fold over both ends and roll up as tightly as you can, to make a neat package. Repeat to make the remaining rolls. Cover with some lettuce leaves to keep them moist (most other things will stick) and chill for up to 4 hours.

For the sauce, pound together the chilli and garlic in a pestle and mortar. Mix with the remaining dressing ingredients and 2 tablespoons of water.

To serve, cut the rolls in half and arrange them on a plate so that they sit upright, with the dipping sauce in a bowl to hand around.

Soups

The words cleansing, balancing and pure spring to mind when I think of eating Asian soups. A bowl of steaming hot and sour broth, subtly flavoured with a perfect balance of aromatics can both satisfy and lift you at the same time. Equally, a pan of Pumpkin, Coconut & Peanut Soup, low-fat Creamy Chicken & Sweetcorn Soup or Shiitake Mushroom Soup offers the creaminess and comfort we all crave at times but without the rather less-good-for-you addition of lots of butter, cream or milk.

Noodles are always popular in my family and we will often make a big pot of Vietnamese Pho as a Saturday lunchtime treat to slurp up! Choosing rice noodles or buckwheat are better options than egg noodles, and soups are pretty adaptable to these changes.

Soups are the ultimate healthy food, especially at lunchtime as an alternative to carbohydrate-packed sandwiches, which often don't contain anything massively healthy and leave you feeling bloated. And the great thing is that you can make them ahead of time and keep them in handy portion sizes for busy times.

SPICY ROASTED PUMPKIN, COCONUT & PEANUT SOUP

Pumpkin is a popular vegetable in all parts of Asia and is prepared in a variety of ways - from salads to curries to soups. I tend to use Japanese pumpkin, but butternut squash is a good alternative. It's a healthy eaters' dream as it is naturally wonderfully creamy in texture and makes you feel like you are eating something really rich and bad for you when you aren't! It is also high in fibre and contains potassium, pantothenic acid, magnesium, and vitamins C and E. And squashes are right at the top of the superfood list because they are rich in carotenoids - key nutrients which are thought to be good for preventing certain types of cancer and reducing heart disease.

This quick-to-make soup also has a number of other veg to make it super healthy and nutritious, and if only mildly spiced, it makes a wonderful family recipe. Though the peanuts don't have to be included, they add not only a wealth of extra nutrients but also a wonderful subtle toasted flavour to the soup. You can add them to the recipe or simply chop them and pass them around for sprinkling, to give the creamy soup a crunchy topping.

Serves 4

PER SERVING: 287 cals | 15g fat | 7g sat fat 10.5g protein | 28g carbs | 18g sugar 1.3g salt

2 tablespoons Thai Red Curry Paste (see page 174)
1 large onion, chopped
2 celery sticks, trimmed and sliced
2 large carrots, chopped
800g blue pumpkin or butternut squash (unprepared weight), peeled and cut into 4cm chunks
3 tablespoons roasted unsalted peanuts (optional)
400ml can light coconut milk
500ml low-salt stock
1 tablespoon fish sauce
good squeeze of lime juice
freshly ground black pepper

Heat a large, non-stick pan and add the curry paste. Over a medium heat, add the onion, celery, carrots and pumpkin or butternut and stir-fry for 2–3 minutes. Add most of the peanuts (if using), coconut milk and stock and a good grind of black pepper and bring up to simmering point. Cook for 20–25 minutes, or until all the vegetables are tender.

Transfer the soup to a blender or using a stick blender, whizz the soup until completely smooth. Stir in the fish sauce and lime juice to taste and garnish with the remaining peanuts.

MISO SOUP WITH SILKEN TOFU & WATERCRESS

A beautifully cleansing soup, which, believe it or not, was taught to me by a Japanese woman in the supermarket one day! I got talking to her and she told me about her favourite miso paste (amongst the 14 or so types on the shelf, which were all labelled in Japanese) and the easiest way to make a detoxing soup. So thank you lovely lady, wherever you are. Had I known it was to become a favourite and that I would be putting your recipe in the book, I would have written down your name!

If you can't find the wakame (dried seaweed) and bonito flakes (dried, smoked fish flakes) you can buy dashi granules to make the stock instead. Homemade stock is superior though. If you want the soup to be veggie, try gently simmering dried shiitake mushrooms in the stock for extra flavour and omit the bonito flakes.

Serves 3-4

Per serving (for 4): 52 cals | 2g fat
0.5g sat fat | 5g protein | 4g carbs
0.1g sugar | 1.6g salt

1 strip wakame dried seaweed
4 heaped tablespoons bonito flakes
4 tablespoons white miso paste or 2 tablespoons red miso paste
100g silken tofu, cut into 2cm cubes
good handful watercress, thick stalks removed

Put the seaweed into a pan with 1.25 litres of cold water and leave to soak for 30 minutes.

Place the pan on the hob and bring the water slowly to the boil. Simmer gently for 10 minutes, then remove the seaweed and place on a chopping board. Add the bonito flakes to the water, bring to the boil and then simmer until they fall to the bottom of the pan – about 2-3 minutes. Remove the pan from the heat and set aside for 5 minutes.

Strain the stock through a sieve (discard the bonito flakes) and return the liquid to a clean pan, chop up the seaweed and add it to the pan. Whisk in the miso paste and add it to the pan along with the tofu. Bring up to a simmer, but do not boil, until piping hot, then throw in the watercress and serve.

SOUPS

THAI HOT & SOUR COCONUT SOUP

A beautiful tasting soup that has a gentle heat to it, and is rich and comforting. Leftover shredded chicken, turkey or small cubes of sweet potato can also be added instead of the prawns, if you prefer. Add the sweet potato after the soup has been simmering for 10 minutes, but don't add the cooked shredded poultry until the end. Make 1½ times the recipe if you are serving this as a main course. You could also add some noodles to make it more substantial or add more stock and omit the coconut milk if you want a Tom Yum-style hot and sour broth, as with the variation below. I have used canned straw mushrooms for ease and variety, but if you want to keep the salt to a minimum, then replace with sliced fresh straw or button mushrooms. For a really quick version, use plain chicken stock with ready-peeled prawns, added at the end of cooking.

Serves 3 as a main course or 4 as a starter

(LG) (GF) (DF) (LS)

Per serving (for 4): 172 kcals | 8.5g fat 6.5g sat fat | 17g protein | 6g carbs 4g sugar | 3.3g salt

16 medium-sized raw unpeeled prawns (about 300g)
spray oil
600ml hot homemade chicken or vegetable stock (or good-quality shop-bought stock)
pinch of dried chilli flakes
2 large green chillies, split ¾ way lengthways
5cm piece fresh ginger, peeled and cut into matchsticks
10 green or pink peppercorns, optional
2 lemongrass stalks, halved and bruised using a rolling pin
2 shallots or ½ small onion, sliced
4 kaffir lime leaves, preferably fresh, split in 2 (or use 7 dried)
400ml can light coconut milk
1 large ripe tomato, deseeded and cut into thin-ish wedges
400g can straw mushrooms, drained, rinsed thoroughly and cut in half
2–3 tablespoons fish sauce
2–3 tablespoons lime juice
good handful of coriander leaves

Peel the prawns and remove the thread down their backbone using a sharp knife. Pop the shells and heads into a saucepan sprayed with a little oil and stir-fry for 2–3 minutes over a high heat until the shells turn pink. Add the stock, giving the shells a bash and a stir with a wooden spoon to release their juice. Bring up to a simmer and cook gently with a lid on for 5 minutes or so while you prepare the rest of the soup.

In a large pan, combine the dried and fresh chillies, ginger, peppercorns (if using), lemongrass, shallots and lime leaves. Strain the stock into the pan and discard the shells. Add the coconut milk to the soup and gently bring up to a simmer. Cook gently for 20 minutes, then add the tomato, mushrooms and prawns and simmer for 5 minutes or so until the prawns are cooked. Add the fish sauce and lime juice and then taste, adding extra of both if required. Ladle into bowls and top with coriander leaves.

Tom Yum Soup: Instead of the coconut milk, increase the quantity of stock by 400ml, making 1 litre.

SHIITAKE MUSHROOM SOUP

Shiitake mushrooms are one of those powerful foods that we should all have more of in our diets. They contain nutrients galore and have been found to boost the immune system and lower cholesterol. Promoters also claim that the lentinan and 1.3 beta glucan they contain actually slow tumour growth and reduce the side effects of cancer treatment – but this is still being studied. Aside from that they are delicious too!

Feel free to use other types of mushroom too – rich portobellos and button mushrooms also marry well with shiitakes. I like to make this with homemade stock (see page 132) or shop-bought fresh, or for a creamier (but not very Asian!) soup, use stock and one-third semi-skimmed milk.

Serves 4

Per serving: 100 cals | 5g fat | 3g sat fat
9g protein | 3g carbs | 2g sugar | 0.6g salt

4 teaspoons coconut or light olive oil
1 medium onion, chopped
2 celery sticks, chopped
2 garlic cloves, crushed
300g shiitake mushrooms, thinly sliced
300g brown chestnut mushrooms, thinly sliced
4 tablespoons Shaoxing Chinese cooking wine or dry sherry
1 teaspoon oyster sauce (optional)
1 litre hot chicken or vegetable stock, or 700ml stock and 300ml
   semi-skimmed milk
2 tablespoons chopped parsley or coriander
salt and freshly ground black pepper

Heat half the oil in a large pan and sauté the onion, celery and garlic with a good pinch of salt, for 8–10 minutes or until soft, then transfer to a bowl and set aside.

Add the remaining oil to the pan and add the mushrooms and another good pinch of salt and a grinding of black pepper. Raise the heat and let the mushrooms brown a little before stirring. When just softened, remove 2 tablespoons of them into a bowl and keep warm, or you can cool them and reheat later in a pan.

Return the onion mix to the pan with the mushrooms and add the wine or sherry. Bubble and stir until evaporated, then add the oyster sauce (if using) and pour in 700ml of the stock, bring to the boil and simmer for 15 minutes.

Transfer the soup to a blender or using a stick blender, whizz the soup until completely smooth. Return the soup to the pan. To keep the soup dairy-free add the remaining stock, otherwise add the milk. Stir in most of the herbs, and mix the remainder with the reserved mushrooms. Divide the soup between 4 warmed bowls and top with the warm herby mushrooms.

CREAMY BUT HEALTHY CHICKEN & SWEETCORN SOUP

Sweetcorn is one of those creamy-textured but healthy ingredients which I turn to when I want a recipe that is rich and comforting but low in fat. You can use canned corn for this soup, but I do prefer it with fresh.

There's not really much to this recipe except the key ingredient, which is the homemade Aromatic Chicken Broth – it's packed with rich flavours and nutrients and makes a fantastic starting point for many soups.

Serves 3 as a main course or 4 as a starter

PER SERVING (FOR 4): 207 cals | 5g fat
1g sat fat | 27g protein | 13g carbs | 1g sugar
0.5g salt

1.1 litres Aromatic Chicken Broth (see page 132) or a full-flavoured fresh chicken stock
2 small corn on the cobs or 150g canned sweetcorn kernels, drained
2 tablespoons cornflour
250g cooked chicken, shredded
squeeze of lemon juice
1 free-range egg, beaten
2 spring onions, shredded
freshly ground black pepper and reduced-salt soy sauce, to taste

Place the stock in a medium pan, bring to the boil and add the fresh corn on the cob (not the canned kernels). Cook for about 10 minutes or until the kernels are soft. Remove the cobs from the pan, and cool slightly. Cut the kernels off the cobs using a sharp knife.

Mix the cornflour with 1–2 tablespoons of cold water and stir gradually into the stock, until it is thickened. Add the fresh or canned corn kernels and shredded chicken to the stock and season to taste with black pepper and soy sauce. Simmer for 5 minutes.

Stir the lemon juice into the beaten egg and just before you are going to serve the soup, use chopsticks to swirl the beaten egg into the pan. Taste for seasoning, then serve immediately scattered with the spring onions.

HEALING 10-MINUTE NOODLES IN BROTH

I have been making subtle variations of this noodle soup for years. It's a wonderful clean-tasting aromatic pick-me-up that can be thrown together with your eyes barely open! It's a zillion times more delicious and better for you than the other alternative for a super-quick soup when you are ill, which I guess would be the opening of a can! I suppose it's a cross between two classic Asian soups, Tom Kha Gai and Laksa.

The crucial components are well-flavoured stock - homemade or shop-bought fresh being preferable to a cube, and at least half the aromatics - the lemongrass, ginger and such. The rest you can wing, depending on what you have in the fridge - add leftover cooked chicken, some prawns, beansprouts, cucumber, pepper, sweetcorn, peas, cabbage or spinach to name a few. Adding coconut milk takes it up a notch and also adds richness, which you may or may not feel like.

Serves 2-3

(LGI) (GF) (DF) (LS) (LF)

PER SERVING (FOR 3): 293 cals | 6g fat
1.5g sat fat | 22g protein | 38g carbs
6.5g sugar | 3g salt

1.25 litres hot chicken stock, or 850ml stock and 400ml can light coconut milk
1 lemongrass stalk, tough outer leaves removed and remaining inner stalk very finely chopped
4cm piece of fresh ginger, peeled and sliced
2 garlic cloves, sliced
½ red chilli, sliced
½ teaspoon clear honey, preferably raw
100g baby corn, halved lengthways
150g sugar snap peas, destrung and cut on the diagonal
100g mushrooms (any type), sliced
4 spring onions, cut into 2.5cm pieces
2 sheets of rice or fine egg noodles, broken in half
2 small pak choi, sliced
1 tablespoon fish sauce
good squeeze of lime juice
freshly ground black pepper and reduced-salt soy sauce, to taste

Pour the stock (and coconut milk, if using), into a large pan and add the lemongrass, ginger, garlic, chilli and honey. Bring slowly up to a simmer and then let it bubble for 2-3 minutes. Throw in all the vegetables, except the pak choi, along with the noodles and cook for 2 minutes, then add the pak choi and simmer for a further minute. Season with the fish sauce and lime juice, then taste and add some black pepper or soy, if needed.

VIETNAMESE PHO

Having rather fallen in love with chef Anthony Bourdain's description of various cafés, bars and restaurants in Ho Chi Minh, I dragged Andrew, my husband, around the city to find various recommended places to eat and drink. The Pho Café was an absolute highlight and made our hunting worthwhile. We arrived to find rows of basic white tables and benches absent-mindedly adorned with the most beautiful table centres – bucketfuls of the freshest, brightest herbs, with smaller dishes of sliced chillies, lime wedges and delicious sauces to choose from. The locals were dotted along the benches all with heads down, slurping away on piping hot bowls of the classic Vietnamese noodle broth. We took our bowls, choosing from chicken or beef (tendon and flank on offer as well as topside) and joined them, plucking leaves and sprinkling chilli to make the soup our own – and it was just perfect.

This is my simplified take on the classic – using an aromatic chicken broth as the base and adding carpaccio-thin raw beef or shredded cooked lean chicken. Even if choosing the beef version (my preference), the chicken stock is so deliciously flavoured that it works as a perfect base for both meats – although a true pho connoisseur would obviously not support me on this!

Serves 4 (LG) (GF) (DF) (LS) (LF)

PER SERVING: 212 cals | 3g fat | 0.5g sat fat
23g protein |22g carbs | 2g sugar | 0.9g salt

200g good-quality raw beef sirloin or fillet, well chilled, or cooked chicken, shredded
1 litre Aromatic Chicken Broth (see page 132)
1 tablespoon fish sauce
100g banh pho noodles, wide flat rice noodles or vermicelli
150g beansprouts, at room temperature

To serve
handful each of Thai basil, coriander and Asian or English chives
4 spring onions, finely shredded
1 long red chilli, thinly sliced
1 lime, cut into wedges
2–3 teaspoons hoisin sauce
2–3 tablespoons sweet chilli sauce or Tabasco sauce

If using beef, cut it into very thin slices, against the grain, with a really sharp knife. Keep the beef at room temperature if using in the next 30 minutes – the piping hot broth essentially cooks the beef, so it's best if it's not fridge cold.

Bring the stock and 200ml of water to the boil, then taste and gradually add the fish sauce until the soup has a good flavour.

Meanwhile, cook the noodles according to the packet instructions. Drain and divide between 4 deep bowls. Top with one-quarter of the beansprouts and one-quarter of the sliced beef or chicken. Add ladlefuls of the piping hot stock and immediately take to the table for guests to add their own toppings. The joy of this soup is that it is eaten DIY-style – so have bowls of washed herbs, spring onions, sliced chilli and lime wedges, as well as some hoisin and sweet chilli sauce in the middle of the table for your guests to add themselves.

Salads & Veggies

Although we associate all salads with being good for us, we can often fall into the trap of thinking they are always a healthy option. We've all said 'I'll just have a salad', but a drizzle of Caesar salad dressing, a rasher or two of crispy bacon, a slice of goat's cheese or a sprinkling of croutons for example, although delicious, can often add extra fat and salt and turn our 'healthy' choice into a more unhealthy one. Not so with Asian salads!

Whether hailing from Vietnam or Thailand, Japan or the Philippines, Asian salads more often than not share the same basic elements – a few simple but super-fresh ingredients – to give them their unique wham bam of crunch, zing and terrific colour, combined with the flavours of fresh herbs and aromatics and a simple but knock-out dressing. You may choose to throw in chicken, prawns or quickly seared beef, and sometimes some fruit, such as pomelo, mango or pineapple to add a burst of freshness. But they always share two things: they are a feast for the eyes and bursting with flavour.

At the heart of a delicious and satisfying Asian salad is the dressing – usually a simple combination of some chilli, a squeeze of lime, a little sweetness and a splash of fish sauce (often without the addition of oil) shaken together in seconds. These intrinsic elements of hot, sour, sweet and salty are at the heart of all South-East Asian cooking, but more noticeable than ever when added to a salad.

ROASTED PUMPKIN WITH ROCKET, TOASTED SEEDS & LEMON MISO DRESSING

A really tasty, hearty salad that can be kept truly Asian if you leave out the rocket, or made more East meets West with the addition of some lamb cutlets on the side or even blanched green beans, feta chunks or black olives stirred into the salad. It can also be made with butternut squash, but the pumpkin takes a little less time in the oven, so check it occasionally during the cooking time to make sure it doesn't go mushy.

Red miso paste is saltier than white, so mix to taste – it depends how strong you like it.

Serves 4 as a main course or 6 as an accompaniment

(V) (GF) (DF) (LS) (LF)

PER SERVING (FOR 6): 86 cals | 5g fat 3g sat fat | 2g protein | 9.5g carbs 6g sugar | 0.2g salt

500g Japanese pumpkin or butternut squash (unprepared weight), peeled and cut into 2.5cm thick wedges or slices
1 tablespoon coconut or light olive oil
2 teaspoons clear honey, preferably raw
pinch of dried chilli flakes
2 teaspoons red or white miso paste
1 ½ tablespoons lemon juice
1 tablespoon extra virgin olive oil
100g rocket
2 heaped teaspoons pumpkin and sunflower seeds
sea salt and freshly ground black pepper

Preheat the oven to 200°C/gas mark 6.

In a baking tray, toss the pumpkin or squash with the coconut oil, half the honey, the chilli flakes and some sea salt and pepper. Bake for 25–35 minutes, or until just tender, adding the seeds for the final 5 minutes. Remove from the oven and set aside to cool.

To make the dressing, in a small jug, whisk the miso paste with the lemon juice, remaining honey and oil. Taste for sweetness and sourness and adjust by adding more oil, miso paste or lemon juice, if necessary.

Transfer the cooled pumpkin or squash and seeds to a serving dish. Add the rocket, drizzle over the dressing and toss to coat.

DAIKON & CARROT SALAD WITH BLACK SESAME SEEDS

Daikon is a superfood that has slipped under the radar for me until now. High in fibre, low in fat and full of vitamin C, potassium and phosphorus it has numerous health benefits. A mandolin or processor with a julienne attachment makes quick work of the vegetable preparation; alternatively a sharp knife will give the same results, but take a little longer. Serve this simple salad with a few pea shoots mixed in for a detoxing salad or for a more substantial main course, add some quickly seared rare tuna, sliced thinly, and a little wasabi on the side, or as an accompaniment to Japanese-style Chicken Burgers (see page 150).

Serves 4 (V) (LGI) (GF) (DF) (LS) (LF)

PER SERVING: 55 cals | 2.5g fat
0.4g sat fat | 1.6g protein | 11g carbs
11g sugar | 0.2g salt

1 daikon or Japanese white radish (about 400g), julienned or finely sliced into 5cm long matchsticks
4 tablespoons rice vinegar
2 carrots, julienned or finely sliced into 5cm long matchsticks
2 teaspoons sesame oil
2 teaspoons clear honey, preferably raw
½ teaspoon grated fresh ginger
1 teaspoon toasted black sesame seeds
salt

Put the daikon in a bowl and sprinkle generously with about 1 teaspoon fine salt and 1 tablespoon of the vinegar. Leave for 10 minutes, then squeeze out really thoroughly and transfer to a bowl of iced water for a further 10 minutes, before draining and squeezing thoroughly again – this removes the bitter taste of the daikon and keeps it crisp.

Mix the daikon with the carrots (use your fingers to separate any clumps of squeezed daikon) in a serving bowl.

In a small jug, mix the remaining ingredients. Pour over the daikon and carrot mix and leave to stand for 30 minutes before serving.

SWEET & SOUR CUCUMBER SALAD

This recipe is a great side dish to serve with salmon, mackerel or other oily fish as it cuts through the richness wonderfully. Traditional Japanese recipes for pickled cucumber salad typically prepare the cucumber in fine ribbons or very thin slices, but I like the added crunch that the slightly thicker slices give, making it more worthy of being called a salad, but it really is up to you.

Serves 6 (V) (LGI) (GF) (DF) (LS) (LF)

PER SERVING: 32 cals | 1g fat | 0.2g sat fat
1g protein | 4.5g carbs | 4.5g sugar
0.6g salt

4 Japanese cucumbers or 2 large English cucumbers (about 600g)
1 ½ teaspoons sea salt flakes
3 teaspoons mild clear honey, preferably raw, or 1g sachet stevia powder
2 tablespoons rice vinegar
2 teaspoons tamari or reduced-salt soy sauce
2 teaspoons toasted black and white sesame seeds

Peel the cucumbers (or you can half peel them by peeling stripes down the lengths), cut them in half lengthways, deseed if using the English cucumbers and then cut into diagonal 5mm slices. Sprinkle with the salt, toss together and leave for 30 minutes in a bowl lined with kitchen paper, for the cucumber to release some of its juice.

Meanwhile, mix all the remaining ingredients together.

After 30 minutes, quickly rinse and pat the cucumber dry, then transfer to a bowl, pour over the dressing and toss together. Taste and add extra honey/stevia if you like. Leave in a cool place or refrigerate for 1 hour before serving.

FIERY GREEN MANGO SALAD

In Singapore we have a lot of mango trees, and they all seem to be laden with fruit around April time. The Filipinos eat the sour green mangoes simply with salt. We have developed a fabulous mango-catching contraption using a net and a metal clothes hanger. I turn a lot of ours into chutney and also make this simple salad – the clean, fiery flavours go beautifully with barbecued squid or prawns or crab cakes, or serve simply as a refreshing starter. Green mangoes are under-ripe mangoes and are high in fibre and packed with vitamins B and C.

The dressing contains dried shrimps – these don't sound very appetising, but rather like adding anchovies to a stew, they add a certain umami flavour to the salad. If you can't find them, just add a little more fish sauce. As this is a classic salty, sour, sweet, hot combo, as in many Thai-inspired recipes, the quantities for the dressing ingredients may need to be adjusted to suit the sourness of the mangoes and the heat of the chillies – the measurements given here can be altered according to taste.

Serves 4 as an accompaniment

(LGI) (DF) (LS) (LF)

Per serving: 135 cals | 2g fat | 0.5g sat fat
4g protein | 26g carbs | 24g sugar
1.7g salt

For the salad

2 under-ripe mangoes (about 600g), peeled, julienned or finely sliced into matchsticks
6 shallots or 1 small red onion, finely sliced
handful of coriander leaves, roughly chopped
8 mint leaves, shredded
1 tablespoon roasted unsalted peanuts (optional)

For the dressing

1 teaspoon dried shrimps (optional)
2 long red chillies, finely sliced (keep the seeds in for fiery heat)
2 tablespoons fish sauce
juice of 2–3 limes
1 teaspoon clear honey, preferably raw, or ½ teaspoon grated palm sugar

Place the mango strips in a bowl of iced water for 5 minutes to crisp.

Meanwhile, for the dressing, grind the shrimps (if using) in a pestle and mortar until they look mashed. Add the chillies, their seeds and the remaining dressing ingredients and pound a little more to combine.

Squeeze the mango over a colander and put into a large bowl with the remaining salad ingredients, pour over the dressing and toss together. Taste and add any extra dressing ingredients as required.

JAPANESE BAKED AUBERGINES

Serve as a starter, lunch or for a vegetarian alternative to the Miso Cod on page 131. The number of aubergine halves this recipe makes depends on the type of aubergine you use – the Japanese variety will give you six halves and the fatter European ones only four, but bigger bits! Therefore, adapt to suit the number of guests, occasion or availability and amend cooking times to suit too – the Japanese variety will cook in 20-25 minutes and the European ones in 35-45 minutes.

Serves 4-6

Per serving (for 6): 41 cals | 1.5g fat
0.1g sat fat | 1.5g protein | 5g carbs
4g sugar | 0.6g salt

3 Japanese long, purple aubergines or 2 European medium, black aubergines (500g), halved lengthways
2 teaspoons coconut or light olive oil
1½-2 tablespoons red or white miso paste (red is saltier, so use less)
2 teaspoons clear honey, preferably raw
2 teaspoons finely grated fresh ginger
1 teaspoon tamari or reduced-salt soy sauce
3 tablespoons mirin
2 spring onion tops, finely chopped or 2 teaspoons toasted sesame seeds

Preheat the oven to 200°C/gas mark 6.

Score the aubergine halves, three-quarters through the flesh, but not through the skin, making diagonal cuts every 1·cm down the flesh.

Brush the aubergines all over with the oil. Transfer to a baking sheet, scored-flesh uppermost, and bake for 20-45 minutes (see introduction) or until the aubergine starts to colour and the flesh is soft and tender.

Meanwhile, mix the miso paste, honey, ginger, tamari or soy and mirin together. Remove the aubergine from the oven.

Preheat the grill to high. Divide the miso sauce between the aubergine halves and spread all over the scored surfaces. Grill on the highest shelf for 3-4 minutes, then sprinkle with the spring onions or sesame seeds and serve.

RAINBOW SLAW WITH PEANUT DRESSING

This salad reminds us of the Yee Sang (prosperity toss) tradition for Chinese New Year, where a colourful salad is placed in the middle of the table and tossed by everyone in turn for good luck.

The peanut dressing is a mellow one compared to some of the other recipes in the book, but as a result, the coleslaw can be happily paired with a collection of other dishes and is a favourite with children too. Feel free to change the dressing to one of the other recipes if you prefer something more refreshing or fiery, as most will go.

If you want to get ahead, make the dressing and keep it chilled in a small jug and prepare the veg and pop it in a large food bag in the fridge earlier in the day. Remove the dressing from the fridge 1 hour before serving, stir well and pour over the veg when ready to serve, so that everything stays crunchy.

Serves 6–8

Per serving (for 8): 109 cals | 7g fat
0.5g sat fat | 4.5g protein | 7g carbs
4.5g sugar | 0.3g salt

For the dressing
1 teaspoon clear honey, preferably raw
3 tablespoons light olive oil
2 teaspoons crunchy peanut butter
1 tablespoon chopped peanuts
1 garlic clove, crushed
1 heaped teaspoon grated fresh ginger
2 teaspoons reduced-salt soy sauce
2 tablespoons rice vinegar
1–2 tablespoons lime juice
salt and freshly ground black pepper

For the salad
150g mangetout or sugar snap peas, destrung and shredded
2 medium carrots, julienned or finely sliced into matchsticks
150g white cabbage, finely shredded
150g red cabbage, finely shredded
1 small red pepper, finely shredded
150g soya or edamame beans, cooked and cooled

For the dressing, put all the ingredients into a small jug with 1 tablespoon of hot water, season and whisk until combined. Taste and adjust if necessary by adding extra lime juice, vinegar, honey or soy sauce.

Put all the vegetables into a serving bowl, and pour the dressing over, toss everything together and serve at once.

WATERCRESS, ASIAN PEAR & MINT SALAD

Simple and refreshing, this crunchy salad is a perfect match to the Asian-style Pork Fillet on page 140 or any barbecued meats. Pears are a great source of fibre, especially present in their skin, along with phytonutrients such as antioxidants, anti-inflammatory flavonoids and potentially anti-cancer cinnamic acids.

Asian pears are less sweet and have a crisp grainy texture. If you can't get hold of Asian pears, then Western pears can be used instead.

Serves 4

Per serving: 98 cals | 5g fat | 0.7g sat fat
2.5g protein | 11g carbs | 10g sugar | 0.1g salt

For the salad
1 heaped tablespoon pumpkin seeds
2 small ripe but firm Asian or Western pears, cored and thinly sliced
2 celery sticks, sliced
handful of small mint leaves
½ English cucumber or 1 Japanese cucumber, halved lengthways and cut into thick slices
100g watercress, trimmed of the thicker stalks

For the dressing
1 tablespoon rice wine vinegar
1 tablespoon light olive oil
1 ½ teaspoons clear honey, preferably raw
flaked sea salt and freshly ground black pepper

Heat a non-stick frying pan over a gentle heat and dry-fry the pumpkin seeds for a minute or so until brown and give off a nutty aroma.

Combine the dressing ingredients in a small jug and whisk together with some flaked sea salt and pepper. Put all the salad ingredients into a bowl and pour the dressing over just before serving. Serve the toasted pumkin seeds on the side.

SUGAR SNAP, SESAME & ORANGE SALAD

A great salad to roll out as an accompaniment to any barbecued meat or fish. The citrus is a great balance to the chargrilled flavours. Cooked quinoa is a delicious and nutritious addition to this salad and gives you the option of not having to serve carbs. However, for a more typically Asian version, leave it out.

Serves 6

Per serving: 123 cals | 5.5g fat
0.7g sat fat | 6g protein | 13g carbs
4.5g sugar | 0.1g salt

200g sugar snap peas, destrung
150g mangetout, destrung
200g asparagus, trimmed
100g quinoa (optional)
2 oranges, peeled and sliced thinly

For the dressing
juice of ½ orange
1 tablespoon red wine or rice vinegar
3cm piece of fresh ginger, peeled and grated
1 teaspoon sesame oil
½ heaped teaspoon Dijon mustard
1 ½ tablespoons light olive oil
2 teaspoons toasted sesame seeds
sea salt
10–15 small mint leaves, to garnish

Bring a large pan of salted water to the boil and blanch the sugar snaps for 1 minute. Drain and transfer to a bowl of iced water or chill under cold running water. Drain thoroughly and set aside. Repeat to blanch the mangetout and asparagus. If using quinoa, add to the boiling vegetable water and cook for 10–12 minutes, then drain and leave to cool.

Whisk together all the dressing ingredients with a good pinch of salt. Arrange the vegetables, oranges and quinoa (if using) on a platter, just before serving. Garnish with the mint and drizzle the dressing over.

SALADS & VEGGIES

REFRESHING PAPAYA & MINT SALAD

One of my favourites, which relies on the all-important balance of sweet, salty, sour and hot to get the flavour of this salad perfect – so taste and adjust until you feel happy with it! For this simple recipe you need to choose papaya that is just 'on the cusp' of being ripe – but still firm. When peeled it should have turned from the paler green unripe colour often seen in Thai salads to a beautiful yellow/orange colour, which has great flavour but a bit more texture to it than the slightly soapy fully ripe papaya that is often left behind on a fruit plate! It looks stunning in a bowl mixed with bright green beans, red chilli and mint leaves and works perfectly with chargrilled squid both as a starter or lunchtime salad and also minus the squid, as an accompaniment to barbecued seafood.

Serves 4 as a starter with squid or as an accompaniment

Per serving (with squid): 124 kcals | 4g fat
0.7g sat fat | 13g protein | 7g carbs
3g sugar | 1.0g g salt

100g green beans, trimmed and cut in half
1 slightly under-ripe papaya
2 shallots (about 50g), finely sliced
2–3 tablespoons mint leaves
300g squid, optional
drizzle of oil, optional

For the dressing
2 tablespoons lime juice (about 1 lime)
1 large red chilli with seeds, finely shredded
1 teaspoon grated palm sugar
1 garlic clove, crushed
1 tablespoon fish sauce

Blanch the green beans for 1 minute in boiling salted water, then refresh in iced water. Peel the papaya, then use a julienne peeler to cut it into strips (you could also thickly grate it into long lengths). Combine all the dressing ingredients in a large bowl and whisk together. Add the papaya, beans, shallots, and mint and toss together.

If planning on serving the salad with squid, prepare the squid as on page 20, but keep as halves rather than cut into smaller pieces. Heat a griddle pan or barbecue, season the squid and drizzle with oil. Chargrill or barbecue for 3–5 minutes on each side. Cut into smaller pieces and serve with the salad.

CHICKEN, PRAWN & POMELO SALAD

The pomelo fruit is like a giant grapefruit, with a very thick, greenish-yellow skin. Unexpectedly though, it has a milder, less astringent taste and slightly drier texture than grapefruit. The two are interchangeable and this recipe is delicious made with pink grapefruit – just go easy on the lime juice as you probably won't need as much.

I tend to use chicken and prawns for a main course salad but if serving as a starter, then I just use prawns. Chunks of avocado are also a delicious addition. Crispy shallots are not the healthiest, but you only need a sprinkling and they add intense flavour. They are available from Asian supermarkets.

Serves 6 as a starter or 4 as a main course

PER SERVING (FOR 6): 176 cals | 7g fat
2.5g sat fat | 21g protein | 6.5g carbs
6g sugar | 1.1g salt

For the dressing
1–1 ½ tablespoons Thai Red Curry Paste (see page 174)
4 tablespoons light coconut milk
1 tablespoon fish sauce
1 teaspoon palm sugar or clear honey, preferably raw
juice of 2–3 limes

For the salad
1 pomelo or 2 pink grapefruit, peeled and segmented or torn into small pieces
200g large cooked and peeled prawns, cut in half crossways
2 poached chicken breasts or 250g cooked chicken, cut into chunks
bunch of coriander, leaves torn
20 Thai or sweet basil leaves, roughly chopped
3 tablespoons roughly chopped roasted, unsalted peanuts
4 spring onions, finely chopped
crispy shallots, to serve (optional)

Dry-fry the curry paste in a small, non-stick pan for 2 minutes. Remove from the heat and whisk in the remaining dressing ingredients, adding the lime juice to taste. Set aside.

Combine all the salad ingredients on a serving platter and toss with the dressing. Serve sprinkled with the crispy shallots (if using).

SIMPLE GREENS WITH GARLIC & OYSTER SAUCE

The wet markets here are chock full of greens, from mild to peppery in flavour. Some are similar to tenderstem broccoli and some are more like cabbage or spinach. Kale and spring greens would also be good alternatives. This recipe uses pak choi, which is easy to locate around the world, but simply slice thicker stalks and add them first if you want to use something else. The mushrooms are also up to you – literally anything goes!

Serves 4 (LGi) (DF) (LS) (LF)

Per serving: 73kcals | 4g fat | 2.5g sat fat
5g protein | 4g carbs | 2.5g sugar | 1.7g salt

1 tablespoon coconut or light olive oil
250g chestnut mushrooms, quartered
2 garlic cloves, sliced
500g pak choi, divided into stems and ends lightly trimmed
1 ½ tablespoons reduced-salt soy sauce
1 ½ tablespoons good-quality oyster sauce
freshy ground black or white pepper

Heat the oil it a wok and throw in the mushrooms. Stir-fry for 1 minute, then add the garlic and cook for a further 1–2 minutes, making sure they don't burn. Add 4 tablespoons of cold water, the pak choi, and the soy and oyster sauces. Season with black or white pepper and stir-fry for a further 4–5 minutes over a medium heat or until the greens are just tender, adding a dash more water to steam-fry the greens if you feel they need it. Serve immediately.

STEAM-FRIED BEANS WITH GARLIC

Beans vary in type in Asia, from the crunchy fine green beans you see in UK supermarkets to the slightly thicker more home-grown type that I remember picking as a child, and of course snake beans/long beans that are much longer and crisper. This recipe is great for cooking any of the thicker varieties, or diagonally cut runner or flat beans too, as the beans are shredded pre-cooking. The added flavour from the garlic and chicken stock makes this a tasty change from normal steaming or boiling.

Serves 4 (LGi) (GF) (DF) (LS) (LF)

Per serving: 65 cals 2g fat | 1.5g sat fat
3g protein | 7g carbs | 6g sugar | 0.9g salt

spray oil, preferably coconut or light olive oil
400g green beans, cut into 5cm long thin diagonal shreds
2 garlic cloves, chopped
200ml hot chicken stock
salt and freshly ground black pepper

Heat the oil in a wok. Add the beans and stir-fry for 2 minutes. Add the garlic and toss in the wok for a further minute. Add the chicken stock, bring to the boil and simmer for 3–4 minutes or until the beans are tender. If using runner beans or thicker beans you might need to cook for a little longer, with a lid on, or add an extra splash of stock if they are drying out. Season, with salt and pepper to taste, and serve immediately.

VIETNAMESE-STYLE CHICKEN SALAD

A super-crunchy salad that is packed with vitamins and very low in fat. It's also quick to rustle up and most accommodating of whatever you have in your fridge. Instead of the suggested ingredients, cherry tomatoes, carrots, shredded cabbage, mangetout and a handful of nuts or seeds are all great additions.

Serves 4

PER SERVING: 214 cals | 4.5g fat
1g sat fat | 28g protein | 15g carbs
14g sugar | 2.5g salt

2 teaspoons sesame seeds
3 tablespoons fish sauce
1 tablespoon rice vinegar
2 tablespoons clear honey, preferably raw
1 red chilli, deseeded and chopped
1 garlic clove, crushed
juice of 1 lime
1 ½ teaspoons sesame oil
150g sugar snap peas or fine green beans, or a mix of both, trimmed or destrung
400g Poached Chicken (page 132) or leftover chicken meat, shredded
2 celery sticks, sliced
1 yellow or red pepper, sliced
175g beansprouts
1 small Japanese or ½ English cucumber, halved lengthways, thickly sliced on the diagonal
4 spring onions, sliced
handful of coriander leaves, chopped
handful of mint leaves, chopped

Heat a small pan and toast the sesame seeds for 1 minute, then add the fish sauce, rice vinegar, honey, chilli, garlic and lime juice to the pan and bring to a simmer. Stir for a further minute or so, then turn off the heat and stir in the sesame oil. Set aside to cool.

Bring a small pan of water to the boil and blanch the sugar snaps for 30 seconds or the beans for 1 minute. Drain and transfer to a bowl of iced water or chill under cold running water. Drain well and transfer to a large serving bowl. Add the chicken, celery, pepper, beansprouts, cucumber, spring onions and herbs. Pour over the dressing and toss together. Serve immediately.

HOT THAI BEEF SALAD

This is an adaptation of a recipe that originally came from the book *Complete Thai Cooking* (Hamlyn). It's been modified over the years to suit different tastes and what's in the storecupboard. But thank you to whoever wrote the original version, as it's a winner. If you like a really feisty sauce, use smaller, punchier chillies or leave the seeds in.

Serves 4

PER SERVING: 290 cals | 8.5g fat
4.5g sat fat | 38g protein | 15g carbs
14.5g sugar | 1.8g salt

2 x 300g thick sirloin steaks, trimmed
juice of 1 lemon
2 tablespoons fish sauce
2 teaspoons coconut or light olive oil
2 long red chillies, deseeded and chopped
2 garlic cloves, finely chopped
100g sugar snap peas
1 large or 2 small ripe but firm mangoes, or 1 large ripe but firm papaya,
    peeled, stoned and cut into 6cm slices
½ English or 1 Japanese cucumber, halved lengthways, deseeded and
    thickly sliced on the diagonal
½ large Chinese cabbage or crunchy lettuce, trimmed, halved and
    shredded or torn into thick pieces
handful of mint leaves, torn

For the dressing
4 large red chillies, deseeded and finely chopped
2 garlic cloves, chopped
2 tablespoons fish sauce
2 teaspoons clear honey, preferably raw
juice of 2 lemons

Place the steaks in a shallow bowl or plastic food bag, add the lemon juice and fish sauce and set aside to marinate for at least 30 minutes or up to 2 hours. Turn the steaks over or give the bag a shake occasionally.

Mix together all the dressing ingredients and set aside.

Heat a heavy-based frying pan over a high heat and add the oil. Remove the steaks from the marinade and scrape any marinade back into the bowl or bag. Fry the steaks for about 3 minutes on each side or until cooked to your liking. Transfer to a chopping board and leave to rest.

Add the chilli and garlic to the pan with the leftover marinade and bring up to the boil. Set aside and keep warm.

In a pan of boiling salted water, blanch the sugar snaps for 1 minute. Drain and transfer to a bowl of iced water or chill under cold running water. Drain and combine with the mango or papaya, cucumber, Chinese cabbage and mint. Slice the beef across the grain into 1cm slices and toss with the warm marinade. Using a slotted spoon, transfer the beef to the salad platter. Pour over half the dressing and toss everything together. Serve immediately with the remaining dressing on the side.

Rice & Noodles

Key to all South-East Asian cuisines and recipes are the many different varieties of rice and noodles consumed by everyone. From a simple bowl of steamed fragrant rice as an accompaniment to a stir-fry or curry to a more complex dish where the rice or noodles are the key component, one or other feature at every Asian mealtime. It is not until I moved to Singapore and wrote a book about grains that I realised both how important and how varied rice is in Asia. My friend, Helen, who comes from the Philippines, explained to me that rice is life or death to the poorer people in her village in the provinces. If a villager can afford two bowls of rice a day they are considered to be managing, if they can't, then they are considered poor and will soon become malnourished.

All varieties of rice or noodles are good for you, but some types are a healthier option. Try buckwheat noodles (which are gluten-free) instead of egg noodles, brown and red rice in place of white. This subtle change will transform a recipe from quite to very nutritious and more often than not, taste better too! White rice and the egg noodles, though providing carbohydrate, won't provide much more, whereas buckwheat or brown rice noodles and brown or red rice will add extra fibre and provide a multitude of vitamins and minerals. Tasty rice salads, stir-fried rice and soba noodles feature virtually daily in our house – although we still enjoy roast potatoes once in a while!

SOBA NOODLE & EDAMAME SALAD WITH PICKLED GINGER DRESSING

This is a delicious salad as it is, but it can also be easily transformed into a more substantial main course with the addition of griddled firm tofu, chicken or salmon. Edamame are high-protein, high-fibre, low-fat, young, soya beans. They also contain good quantities of omega-3 fatty acids. They can be bought fresh and still in their pod (in which case use podded weight) or you can buy them frozen. If you can't find edamame beans use broad beans instead.

Soba noodles are made from buckwheat, which is also rich in proteins, and the amino acid lysine, which is lacking in most cereal grains. Buckwheat is also abundant in lipids, minerals (iron, phosphorus and copper), and vitamins B1 and B2. Green tea soba noodles have the added bonus of the addition of the superfood green tea that is thought to have anti-cancer properties, plus they are a beautiful colour!

The salad is finished with a topping of crisp nori seaweed – I buy mini snack sheets of seaweed which are perfect for snipping and sprinkling over the salad. Sushi nori sheets can also be used, but cut them very finely or they will be too chewy.

Serves 4 (V) (L-G) (DF) (LS) (LF)
PER SERVING: 256 cals | 9g fat | 1g sat fat
9g protein | 35g carbs| 5g sugar | 1.2g salt

For the salad
180g soba noodles or green tea soba noodles
75g frozen edamame beans
100g sugar snap peas, destrung
5 radishes, very thinly sliced

For the dressing
2 tablespoons light olive oil
2 teaspoon sesame oil
3 tablespoons Japanese rice vinegar
1 teaspoon clear honey, preferably raw
1 tablespoon tamari or reduced-salt soy sauce
1 tablespoon finely chopped pickled ginger or ½ teaspoon
    grated fresh ginger
½ sheet crisp nori seaweed, cut into fine strips with scissors

Cook the noodles according to the packet instructions until just tender, stirring the noodles once (when wilted), to prevent them sticking together.

Bring a medium pan of water to the boil and add the frozen edamame beans. Bring back up to the boil, then add the sugar snap peas and cook for 1 minute. Drain the noodles and vegetables and transfer to a bowl of iced water to cool, or chill under cold running water before draining again. Slice the sugar snaps in half diagonally and place in a serving bowl with the beans, noodles and radishes.

Mix all the dressing ingredients together in a small jug. Pour half the dressing over the noodle mixture and toss well to combine. Cover and chill for 2 hours.

Toss the noodles with the remaining dressing and top with the shredded nori, to serve.

RICE & NOODLES

PAD THAI NOODLES

Veggie or not, the option is yours. We ate the best Pad Thai stir-fried rice noodles when staying in Krabi, Thailand. The secret ingredient was a dash of a bitter cherry sauce, which I brought home and kept in my fridge. Sadly, it's now run out, hence using tamarind as an alternative. Thais often wrap the noodles in a square blanket of omelette, rather than adding beaten egg to the mixture, which looks pretty and keeps them warm. The quantity of noodles does rather vary depending on which ones you use, so feel free to add more or less, depending on how they look once soaked.

Serves 4

Per serving (with 300g tofu): 511 cals
23g fat | 10g sat fat | 22g protein
51g carbs| 10g sugar | 2.3g salt

200g medium rice noodles
2 ½–3 tablespoons coconut or light olive oil
3 free-range eggs, beaten
1 teaspoon reduced-salt soy sauce
150g firm tofu (or use 300g if not including meat or prawns), cut into 2cm cubes
250g medium raw prawns, peeled and deveined (about 500g unpeeled weight) or 2 chicken breasts, thinly sliced, or a mix of both (optional)
2 garlic cloves, chopped
2 good pinches of cayenne pepper or ½ teaspoon of dried chilli flakes
2 teaspoons ground dried shrimps (optional)
100g beansprouts
3 spring onions, trimmed and finely chopped

For the sauce
2 tablespoons tamarind paste or purée (see Tip on page 92)
2 tablespoons fish sauce
1 ½ teaspoons palm sugar or honey, preferably raw
1 heaped tablespoon tomato ketchup
1–2 tablespoons lime juice

To serve
3 heaped tablespoons roasted peanuts, finely chopped
Lime wedges and 2 heaped tablespoons chopped coriander

You can prepare the noodles first and keep them moist by tossing them in a teaspoon of mild oil. You will then be ready to quickly stir-fry everything. To do this, put the noodles in a large bowl, cover with plenty of boiling water and leave to soften for 10 minutes. Drain and rinse in cold water before tossing with 1 teaspoon of the oil.

Meanwhile, mix all the sauce ingredients together in a small bowl. Beat the eggs with the soy sauce and prepare all the other ingredients.

Heat 2 teaspoons of the oil in a wok and stir-fry the tofu for 5–6 minutes over a medium heat. It does break up a little during cooking but don't worry too much about that. Remove with a slotted spoon and transfer to a plate lined with kitchen paper. Add another teaspoon of oil to the wok and stir-fry the prawns or chicken (or cook the chicken followed by the

Recipe continues overleaf...

prawns if using both) for 3–4 minutes, adding the garlic for the final minute, until cooked through. Remove to a plate.

Heat 1 teaspoon of the oil in a frying pan, pour in the eggs and cook for a minute or so to make a large thin omelette. Flip over, cook for a further few seconds, then slide onto a board and chop.

Heat the final splash of oil in the wok and add the drained noodles. Stir-fry over a high heat until piping hot, then add the sauce, chicken and prawns (if using), as well as the cayenne pepper or chilli and dried shrimps. Toss over the heat, then add the sauce and beansprouts and toss together again untill the noodles are coated. Throw in the spring onions and chopped omelette, give everything a final toss before pouring onto a platter and topping with the peanuts, tofu and coriander. Serve with lime wedges.

RICE & NOODLES

HEALTHY FRIED RICE

Fried rice is our 'go to' for a mid-week family supper or Saturday lunch. Though the name suggests otherwise, it needn't have lots of oil in it – just enough to lightly coat the grains and give them a lovely toasty flavour. This is what I think of as a storecupboard recipe: it is versatile and you can add any number of other bits and bobs you have handy in the fridge. I have kept this version veggie but it can easily be made more substantial with the addition of a couple of handfuls of defrosted cooked prawns, ham, cold roast pork or some bacon, chicken breast or thigh meat, chopped, stir-fried and set aside at the beginning and then thrown back in to the rice mixture for the final 2–3 minutes of cooking. It is very important that the rice is not overcooked but just tender, and it should be really cold, so the grains have dried out a little before you stir-fry them.

Serves 4

PER SERVING: 335 cals | 10g fat | 4g sat fat
12g protein | 51g carbs | 4.5g sugar
0.9g salt

3 teaspoons coconut oil
1 large carrot, chopped into 1cm cubes
100g mangetout or sugar snap peas, sliced diagonally into 2cm pieces
100g baby corn, sliced diagonally
600g cooked (300g raw) basmati rice, chilled
3 free-range eggs, lightly beaten
1–2 tablespoons reduced-salt soy sauce
3 large spring onions, finely sliced
4 tablespoons frozen peas, defrosted
salt and white pepper

Heat 1 teaspoon of the oil in a non-stick wok. Stir-fry the carrot, mangetout or sugar snap peas and baby corn for 3 minutes. Be careful not to overcook them – they should still have a slight crunch. Transfer the vegetables to a large plate and set aside.

Add the remaining oil to the wok and heat until smoking hot. Add the rice and toss thoroughly in the oil so that all the individual grains get a good coating. Push the rice aside to leave space to cook the egg in the bottom of the wok. Turn down the heat slightly, season the beaten egg, pour into the wok and let it set – it should resemble a partially cooked omelette. Break the egg up and combine it with the rice so that the egg is evenly distributed. Add the soy sauce and pepper to taste, followed by the cooked vegetables and the spring onions and peas. Stir well to combine and ensure everything is piping hot, and let the rice just start to brown on the bottom of the pan as it will give it a delicious toasty flavour. If the rice seems too dry, add a little water towards the end but no earlier or the rice will become stodgy. Taste for seasoning, adding a little more soy sauce if needed.

SOBA NOODLE SALAD WITH GRIDDLED LIME CHICKEN

This is a great salad with a versatile dressing that appeals to young and old. Buckwheat soba noodles are delicious, gluten-free and certainly more nutritious than egg noodles, but you can easily swap to the latter if you prefer. Egg noodles tend to really soak up the dressing though, so make double the quantity of dressing if you do use them.

You can poach the chicken in advance (see page 132) if you prefer, and serve the whole dish cold, but personally, I like to griddle or barbecue the chicken breasts and serve the salad warm or at room temperature rather than cold.

Serves 4-6

Per serving (for 6): 328 cals | 12g fat 1.7g sat fat | 25.3g protein | 30g carbs 6g sugar | 1.3g salt

3 chicken breasts
2 teaspoons sesame oil
2 teaspoons reduced-salt soy sauce
juice of 1 lime
1 teaspoon grated fresh ginger
225g soba noodles
1 large carrot, julienned or thickly grated
½ red pepper, thinly sliced
½ yellow pepper, thinly sliced
100g beansprouts
bunch of coriander, leaves chopped
2 spring onions, chopped

For the dressing
1 teaspoon clear honey, preferably raw
3 tablespoons light olive oil
2 teaspoons crunchy peanut butter
1 tablespoon chopped roasted peanuts
1 garlic clove, crushed
1 heaped teaspoon grated fresh ginger
2 teaspoons reduced-salt soy sauce
2 tablespoons rice vinegar
juice of 1 lime
salt and freshly ground black pepper

Put the chicken breasts onto a chopping board between two sheets of baking parchment and bash with a rolling pin until flattened to about 2cm thick. In a non-metallic shallow dish combine the sesame oil, soy sauce, lime juice and ginger. Place the chicken in the dish and spoon the marinade over. Chill in the fridge to marinate for up to 4 hours.

Combine all the dressing ingredients in a jug with 2 tablespoons of hot water, season and whisk together until combined. Taste and adjust the seasoning, if needed. Leave in the fridge until 20 minutes or so before you want to use it (it will need a good stir).

Heat a griddle or barbecue to very hot. Add the chicken and cook for 3-4 minutes on each side and leave to rest, covered loosely with foil, for 5 minutes. Meanwhile, cook the noodles according to the packet instructions, stirring the noodles once (when wilted), to prevent them sticking together. Then drain, and leave to cool for 5 minutes.

Whisk the dressing to combine, then pour over the noodles and toss together with the carrot, peppers, beansprouts and most of the coriander. Spoon the noodles onto a platter, slice the chicken and arrange down the centre, then sprinkle with the spring onions and remaining coriander.

NO-COOK
ONE-POT NOODLES

I can't take the credit for this inspired idea as similar has been done before. However, there are numerous variations and I think the world needs to know that a boring office lunch needn't be eaten ever again! It's a simple concept – no-cook rice noodles, finely shredded vegetables or some shredded cooked chicken, and a delicious sachet or spoonful of super-healthy and cleansing miso soup. All you need is a kettle of boiling water and 10 minutes. My only slight tweak is that I find that if you 'cook' your veg in the miso soup, by the time you eat it it's lukewarm. This is an easy problem to solve with a microwave or do as I've suggested in the recipe and pour some freshly made soup over the soaked, drained noodles. Feel free to swap another flavoured Asian soup or broth to pour over as the miso is not to everyone's taste.

Serves 1

Per serving (for basic noodle soup):
249 cals | 2.5g fat | 0.5g sat fat | 10g protein
43g carbs | 3g sugar | 2.5g salt

For the basic noodles

40g fine rice vermicelli noodles, broken up a bit (I use brown rice ones, which take 10 minutes to cook)
handful of beansprouts
small handful of finely shredded Chinese leaves, spinach or pak choi
2 spring onions, finely sliced
small handful of mangetout or sugar snap peas, shredded, or frozen peas
1 packet instant miso soup (preferably low-salt)

Optional extras

50g silken tofu, cubed
4 cooked tiger prawns, halved (keep in the fridge until you need them)
handful of cooked chicken, shredded (keep in the fridge until needed)
50g enoki mushrooms
handful of steamed small broccoli florets or halved baby corn
1 tablespoon chopped coriander leaves
½ small carrot, grated
squeeze of lime juice

Take a heatproof container with a lid – this could be a microwave bowl, plastic food container, a food flask or even a jam jar. Put the noodles and vegetables into the container and carry to work, along with the sachet of miso soup mix.

When ready to eat, simply remove the soup sachet, pour some just-boiled water over the noodles and vegetables to just cover and leave for 10 minutes, before draining off as much of the water as possible.

Make up the soup with freshly boiled water following the packet instructions. Pour over the noodles and veg and any optional extras, stir and eat immediately.

STIR-FRIED SPICY NOODLES

There are many types of noodle dishes sold in the wet markets and hawker stalls of Asia – with a variety of types and thickness of noodles used: some are soupy, some dry and generally all are delicious! Wonton Mee (noodles with wontons), Laksa (noodles in curry sauce), Hokkein Mee (egg and rice noodles with pork and seafood), Char Kway Teow (fried flat noodles) are just some of the ones I've tried since living in Asia. Though mostly very tasty, they are often extremely high in salt and fat – and are not to be eaten on a regular basis! Interestingly, I've not found a dish of Singapore noodles so far. To research a little further, I recently read an article all about Singapore noodles, which confirmed that they are in fact a Cantonese dish and not from Singapore at all – though there is obviously a strong Chinese influence to much of the cooking here. This spicy noodle dish is a bit of a mix of influences – similar to the Filipino Bihon, a nod to what we know as Singapore noodles, and a generally healthier take on the noodles sold at the hawker centres. I find that adding some fresh chilli and curry powder as well as a good squeeze of fresh lime gives so much flavour without the addition of loads of nasties, which can often leave you feeling very thirsty and heavy!

Serves 2–3 (LG) (GF) (DF) (LS) (LF)

PER SERVING (FOR 3): 336 cals | 6g fat
2.3g sat fat | 28.7g protein | 36.7g carbs
2.6g sugar | 1.5g salt

100g rice vermicelli noodles
2 teaspoons coconut or light olive oil
1 small red onion, sliced
1 green chilli, with seeds, finely sliced
2 garlic cloves, sliced
5cm piece fresh ginger, peeled, sliced and cut into thin matchsticks
½ yellow pepper, thinly sliced
5 shiitake mushrooms, sliced
4 water chestnuts, sliced
125g cooked pork, chopped
125g medium to large peeled and deveined raw prawns (about 250g unpeeled weight), cut into 1cm lengths, or handful frozen, cooked smaller prawns, defrosted
1 free-range egg, beaten
2 tablespoons Shaoxing Chinese cooking wine or dry sherry
1–2 tablespoons reduced-salt soy sauce
1 teaspoon hot curry powder or paste
½ teaspoon ground turmeric
125g beansprouts
1–2 tablespoons lime juice
good handful coriander leaves, roughly chopped
salt and white pepper

Soak the noodles in a large bowl of salted boiling water for 10 minutes, then drain.

Heat half the oil in a wok and gently stir-fry the onion for 2 minutes. Add the chilli, garlic, ginger and pepper and stir-fry over a medium heat for a further 2–3 minutes. Add the mushrooms and water chestnuts and stir-fry for 2 minutes, then add the pork and prawns and toss over the heat for 1 minute.

Push everything to one side, season the beaten egg and pour it in to the wok. Let it set in the bottom of the pan, then break it up using a spatula, then mix with the other ingredients in the wok. Pour in the wine and 1 tablespoon of the soy sauce and bubble until reduced.

Mix the curry powder and turmeric with the drained noodles. Increase the heat and add the remaining oil, noodles and beansprouts to the wok. Toss together adding a pinch of salt and a sprinkling of white pepper. Add half the lime juice and the coriander and toss again. Taste and add extra soy sauce or lime juice, if needed.

ASIAN BROWN RICE SALAD

This is an adaptation of my Australian friend Maree's 'go to' rice salad recipe. It's dead simple, with the lovely crunchy textures and toasty flavours of nuts and seeds and a refreshing zing from the currants. What's extra good about it is that it's packed with vitamins and minerals and benefits from being made the day before - just stir in the parsley before serving. We now make this slightly adapted version of the original all the time as it's a great accompaniment to barbecued lamb or anything straight from the grill and is easily transportable to other people's houses!

Serves 8-10 as an accompaniment

(V) (VE) (LG) (GF) (DF) (LS) (LF)

Per serving (for 10): 268 cals | 12g fat 1.5g sat fat | 5g protein | 35.5g carbs 9g sugar | 0.4g salt

For the dressing
3 tablespoons tamari or reduced-salt soy sauce
3 tablespoons lemon juice
3 tablespoons light olive oil
1 large or 2 small garlic cloves, crushed
2 heaped teaspoons grated fresh ginger
large bunch of parsley, leaves removed and chopped
salt and freshly ground black pepper

For the salad
800g (400g raw) just-cooked brown basmati rice
3 tablespoons pine nuts
3 tablespoons cashew nuts
2 tablespoons sunflower seeds
1 tablespoon linseeds
150g green beans, trimmed
6 spring onions, finely sliced
1 large red pepper, chopped into 2cm dice
100g currants or dried cranberries

Whisk together all the dressing ingredients (omit the parsley at this stage, if making in advance, and add just before serving) and season to taste. Place the warm rice in a large bowl and stir the dressing in. Leave to cool completely.

In a dry frying pan, lightly brown the nuts and sunflower seeds, so that they release their toasty flavour. Leave to cool, then roughly chop the cashew nuts and add the nuts, sunflower seeds and linseeds to the rice.

Bring a small pan of salted water to the boil and blanch the green beans for 1 minute. Drain and transfer to a bowl of iced water or chill under cold running water. Chop the beans into 2cm pieces and add to the rice, along with the spring onions, red pepper and dried fruit. Mix together and leave covered in the fridge until ready to eat.

RICE & NOODLES

NONYA RICE SALAD

The term Nonya or Nyonya is used to describe the cuisine of Peranakans – descendants of early Chinese migrants who settled in Penang, Malacca, Indonesia and Singapore, inter-marrying with local Malays. This recipe is a variation of a cold rice salad called Nasi Ulam, a staple in Nonya cuisine. There are many interpretations, but the Malay version consists of rice mixed with shredded herbs, such as betelnut leaf and cashew leaf shoots, pounded toasted coconut, spices, and sometimes shredded fried fish is mixed in. It has powerful flavours and packs a punch. I have tweaked and fiddled and have come up with my own version, which omits the tricky-to-find Asian ingredients and adds the health benefits of using red rice. I love the addition of sugar snaps for crunchiness, but I also like to use the popular Asian raw winged beans as they look so beautiful and have the same pea-like freshness. I rinse the rice thoroughly and then leave it to soak for 15 minutes before cooking it in boiling salted water for about 25 minutes or until tender.

Serves 4 as a main course or
6 as an accompaniment

(L-G) (DF) (LS) (LF)

Per serving (for 6): 157 cals | 6g fat
5g sat fat | 5.5g protein | 20g carbs
2g sugar | 0.4g salt

For the paste

25g dried whole shrimps
3 red chillies, with seeds, sliced
2 garlic cloves, roughly chopped
50g shallots

For the salad

3 tablespoons shredded or grated coconut
600g cooked (300g raw) red rice, chilled
2 teaspoons coconut or light olive oil
2 lemongrass stalks, tough outer leaves removed and remaining inner stalks very finely chopped
150g sugar snap peas, trimmed and shredded into 5mm strips
4 fresh kaffir lime leaves, finely shredded, or the zest of 2 unwaxed limes
2 heaped tablespoons chopped coriander
2 heaped tablespoons chopped mint
2 heaped tablespoons chopped Thai basil
juice of 2–3 limes
salt and freshly ground black pepper

Start by making the paste. Put the shrimps into a bowl with 3 table-spoons of boiling water and leave to soak for 30 minutes. Drain and put into a mini processor with the chillies, garlic and shallots and blend to a coarse paste.

Heat a small frying pan and quickly dry-fry the coconut until it is pale brown (watch it as it literally turns in seconds). Transfer to a bowl with the cooked rice. Heat the oil in the same pan and add the lemongrass. Cook gently for a few seconds before adding the paste and frying for 1–2 minutes only – just to take away the raw edge – then transfer to the bowl with the rice. Add the sugar snap peas, limes leaves or lime zest, herbs and lime juice and toss together. Taste for seasoning and serve.

PRAWN, BROWN RICE & TENDERSTEM STIR-FRY

Brown rice is a great high-fibre, low-GI alternative to white rice and it has more nutrients as it is unprocessed. It gives a delicious nuttiness to fried rice. Make sure that the rice you are using is cooked at least 3-4 hours ahead – (it should be just tender rather than soft), so that is has the chance to get totally fridge cold. I cook it and then spread it over a plate to get rid of all the steam and separate the grains.

Tenderstem broccoli is one of my favourite vegetables as it's a cross between asparagus, greens and broccoli and is packed full of vitamins too. However, you can use pak choi or kai lan for a more Asian equivalent. This dish is loosely based on the popular recipe, Nasi Goreng. Traditionally, it would be served with a fried egg on top, but I will leave that decision to the chef! Don't be stingy on the prawns, as they add great texture and flavour. A 250g or so bag of frozen, then defrosted raw prawns will also do if you can't buy fresh or they are too expensive.

Serves 4

PER SERVING: 244 cals | 4g fat | 2g sat fat 17g protein | 35g carbs | 3g sugar 1.1g salt

24 medium raw prawns, peeled and deveined
3 teaspoons reduced-salt soy sauce
1 large bunch (about 450g) tenderstem broccoli or kai lan, ends trimmed
5 teaspoons coconut or light olive oil
1 medium onion, chopped
12 shiitake or 8 brown button mushrooms, sliced
½–1 long red chilli, deseeded and chopped (optional)
2 garlic cloves, sliced thinly
3–5 tablespoons chicken or vegetable stock or water
600g cooked (300g raw) basmati rice, chilled
2–3 tablespoons oyster sauce
2 spring onions, finely chopped
1 tablespoon chopped coriander
ground white pepper

Place the prawns in a bowl with 1 teaspoon of the soy sauce. Cut the broccoli stems into 4cm pieces and keep the florets whole.

In a large, preferably non-stick wok, heat 1 teaspoon of the oil over a medium heat and stir-fry the onion until starting to soften. Add the mushrooms, chilli (if using) and garlic to the wok and stir-fry over a high heat for 2 minutes, so that the garlic and mushrooms are just cooked. Transfer to a large bowl and set aside.

Add a further teaspoon of oil and heat until smoking hot. Add the prawns and stir-fry for a couple of minutes until they have turned pink, then transfer to the bowl with the onion and mushrooms.

Add another teaspoon of oil and the broccoli to the wok, stir-fry for a minute before adding 3-4 tablespoons of the stock or water to let the broccoli steam. Toss until the stems are just tender yet still crunchy, then transfer to the bowl with the prawns and onions.

Heat the remaining 2 teaspoons oil in the wok until smoking, then add the cold rice and toss together for 1 minute. Add the onion, mushrooms, garlic, broccoli and prawns and their juices to the wok, along with 2 tablespoons of the oyster sauce, the spring onions, the remaining 2 teaspoons of soy sauce and some white pepper. Stir-fry together until combined and the rice is piping hot. Taste for seasoning, adding a little more oyster sauce, stock or pepper if needed. Sprinkle with the coriander and serve immediately.

CHICKEN, MANGO & RICE SALAD

I think we probably eat this, or a variation of it, once every two weeks, and the children also have it in their packed lunches too – but minus the chilli and with the addition of some cucumber. However, it's a great salad for larger numbers too. To poach the chicken see page 132. I'm a fan of using a rainbow of grains as you get both colour and a wider variety of nutrients.

Serves 6

PER SERVING: 377 cals | 17g fat
7g sat fat | 29g protein | 29g carbs
7.5g sugar | 0.9g salt

100g green beans, cut into 5cm lengths
4 poached chicken breasts, sliced, or 500g cooked chicken, shredded
400g cooked and chilled (200g raw) brown, red or white basmati rice, or a mixture
1 large ripe mango, peeled and cubed
3 spring onions, finely shredded
juice of 2 limes
1 ½ tablespoons coconut or light olive oil
1 ½ tablespoons fish sauce
1 large red chilli, deseeded and chopped (optional)
3 tablespoons shredded or desiccated coconut
1 ripe, firm avocado, cubed
bunch of coriander, leaves roughly chopped
handful of mint leaves, torn
3 handfuls of baby spinach, torn
freshly ground black pepper

In a pan of boiling salted water, blanch the green beans for 1–2 minutes so they are cooked but still crunchy. Drain and transfer to a bowl of iced water or chill under cold running water.

Carefully combine all the other ingredients, except the avocado, herbs and spinach, on a large platter and toss together. Leave for 15 minutes.

Just before serving, add the remaining ingredients and a good grinding of pepper and toss together carefully.

Stir-fries

Arriving at the bustling vibrant market first thing in the morning is a joy for the senses. My favourite way to shop has always been to be unplanned! Just pottering around a market is so much more fun than trolley rage in the local supermarket as busy customers rush to fulfil their shopping list and get out as quickly as possible – although sadly I still have to do that too!

Market stallholders in Singapore love to be asked what's fresh in that morning or newly in season, which fruits taste the sweetest or how things are best prepared. If you take your time, you can learn so much from those that work there and I find there's always a new fish or herb or vegetable to take home and try – I think of it as my homework.

Our local market at Empress never fails to please and people-watching is always an added bonus, too, as Singaporeans really love their food. The older Singapore ladies know what they want, often ignoring queues and always being hands-on feeling and sniffing until they are satisfied that they have the best. The same goes for the farmers' markets in the UK or Australia – take advice from the experts, choose what's just been picked and prepare it simply to taste it at its best.

A stir-fry is the perfect post-market food to cook as it needs little more than the freshest, tastiest ingredients, chopped according to their cooking time and then quickly steam-fried in a wok as quickly as possible. I'm not a great fan of the gloopy, sweet and salty sauces that are often added to stir-fries and prefer to let the ingredients shine with an easy marinade or light touch of flavouring added at the end of cooking. The key to successful stir-frying is to always have everything chopped or marinated ahead of time so you can keep the heat high, the wok moving and the nutrients intact.

STIR-FRIED PRAWNS WITH TAMARIND & CORIANDER DRESSING

This is a sort of stir-fry-cum-salad, as the hot dressed prawns should be tossed with the crunchy leaves and herbs and served immediately. It can also be served as a starter.

Tamarind is one of my favourite ingredients in Asian cooking. It can be bought fresh in Singapore, in pods which contain a pulpy paste and seeds. If bought as a harder block you need to add a little boiling water and once spoonable squish it through a sieve to catch the seeds. The tangy flavour is a marvellous addition to stir-fries and sauces and it is said to have a massive amount of natural medicinal benefits, such as aiding digestive problems, lowering fevers and soothing sore throats.

Serves 3–4 as a main course or 6 as a starter

Per serving (for 4): 122 cals | 6g fat
5g sat fat | 11g protein | 6g carbs
6g sugar | 0.4g salt

For the dressing

40g coriander, leaves picked and thick stems discarded
1 long red chilli, deseeded and chopped
1 garlic clove, crushed
2 tablespoons tamarind paste or purée (see Tip)
2 teaspoons clear honey, preferably raw
1 tablespoon lime juice
2½ tablespoons coconut or light olive oil

For the salad

175g mixed baby spinach, rocket and watercress
25g small mint leaves
½ tablespoon coconut or light olive oil
325g large raw prawns, peeled and deveined, keep the tails on
   (650g unpeeled weight)
crusty bread, to serve

Put all the dressing ingredients into a mini blender and whizz until puréed. Alternatively, very finely chop the coriander, chilli and garlic and whisk together in a bowl with the other ingredients.

In a large serving dish mix together the salad leaves and mint.

Heat the oil in a wok until hot, add the prawns and stir-fry for 2 minutes or so until just cooked. Add the dressing and toss over the heat for a minute. Spoon the prawns and dressing over the leaves, toss together and serve immediately with crusty bread.

Tip: Tamarind is sometimes sold as a block. To make it into a purée, put approximately 2 tablespoons of the tamarind into a bowl with 1–2 tablespoons of boiling water. Using a spoon, squash it together until it forms a purée and then pass it through a sieve. It should have the consistency of melted chocolate.

STEAM-FRIED VEGETABLES

Additional flavours to add to this simple cleansing stir-fry are endless, as are variations on veggies or the addition of some sliced firm tofu, thinly sliced lean beef or chicken. Simply cook the meat for a minute or so in the oil and transfer to a plate before adding with the pak choi for the final few minutes. A little black bean sauce, some chilli sauce or some yellow bean paste all work well in place of the sauce shown here (just avoid the high-salt and high-sugar ones like sweet and sour and ensure you buy a good-quality brand without additives). Tips for stir-frying: cut the veg to match their cooking time (slice tougher vegetables such as carrot thinner than, say, baby corn for example and remember to steam-fry (adding a splash of water or stock whilst you fry to avoid charred edges and keep in control of your cooking).

Serves 4 as a main or
8 as an accompaniment

(DF) (LF)

PER SERVING: 116 cals | 4g fat | 0.5g sat fat
5.5g protein | 15g carbs | 13g sugar | 2.7g salt

1 tablespoon coconut or light olive oil
½ large onion, sliced into thinnish wedges
2 carrots, peeled and thinly sliced on the diagonal
2 garlic cloves, sliced
½ red chilli, finely chopped
150g shiitake or chestnut mushrooms, quartered
200g mangetout, trimmed
6 spring onions, cut into 2cm slices
350g pak choi, separated into leaves, or ⅓ Chinese cabbage, thickly sliced
ground white pepper

For the sauce
4 tablespoons weak vegetable or chicken stock
2 tablespoons fish sauce, or to taste
2 tablespoons reduced-salt soy sauce
1 tablespoon lime juice, or to taste
1 tablespoon clear honey, preferably raw

Mix the sauce ingredients together.

Heat the oil in a large wok and add the onion and carrots. Stir-fry gently for 3 minutes, then add the garlic and chilli and cook for a further 1–2 minutes. Turn the heat up to medium, then add the mushrooms and stir-fry for 1 minute, then add the mangetout and a dash of water (1–2 tablespoons max) and cook for 1–2 minutes to 'steam-fry'. Add the spring onions, pak choi or cabbage, along with the sauce and some white pepper and cook briefly, until the leaves are just wilted. Serve immediately.

THAI-STYLE STUFFED OMELETTE WITH WILTED SPINACH AND PEPPERS

This to me is simple comfort food. The omelette is a delicious lunch in itself and a tasty change from the usual style, but the vegetable filling makes it a more substantial dish, so delicious and perfect for vegetarians too – if you just substitute the fish sauce with soy sauce, and use vegetarian oyster sauce. Other fillings could include endless other stir-fry veg, crab, ginger and chilli, or minced pork and vegetables.

Serves 2 (DF)(LS)

PER SERVING: 228 cals | 15g fat | 4g sat fat
17g protein | 6.5g carbs | 6.5g sugar | 2g salt

For the filling
spray oil
½ red or yellow pepper, cut into 2cm chunks
2 spring onions, cut into 4cm pieces
1 garlic clove, thinly sliced
1 tomato, deseeded and roughly chopped
6 shiitake or button mushrooms, thinly sliced
3 big handfuls of baby spinach, stalks removed
1 teaspoon reduced-salt soy sauce
1 teaspoon hoisin sauce or 2 teaspoons oyster sauce
freshly ground black pepper

For the omelettes
4 free-range eggs
2 teaspoons fish sauce
1 tablespoon chopped coriander
2 spring onions, finely sliced

Spray a little oil into a wok and add all the vegetables, except the spinach. Stir-fry for 2–3 minutes, then add a splash of water and steam-fry for 1–2 minutes or until the pepper chunks are crunchy but just tender. Add the spinach and stir until wilted. Add the soy sauce and hoisin or oyster sauce and a good grinding of black pepper. Keep warm in a low oven.

Whisk the eggs with the fish sauce, coriander and spring onions in a jug. Heat a spray of oil in a small omelette pan, add half the egg mixture and cook until just set. Using a spatula or palette knife, carefully flip over and when just done, slide onto a plate. Repeat with the remaining mixture to make a second omelette. Alternatively, use a large frying pan or the wok used to cook the vegetables and make one large omelette – cook one side, slide it onto a plate and then flip the plate over so the omelette goes back in the pan, raw-side down.

Divide the warm filling between the two small omelettes or large omelette and fold over. Halve the large omelette, transfer to plates and serve immediately.

CAMBODIAN SQUID WITH GREEN PEPPERCORNS

We ate a variation of this when on holiday in Kep, Cambodia, made with the local fresh Kampot green peppercorns, which are added still on their stems. Their flavour is wonderfully delicate and almost sweet as well as mildly peppery – delicious! The green soaked peppercorns in brine are the nearest I can find to the fresh ones, but if you'd like more punch, then pink peppercorns are stronger.

If you can only buy thicker squid rather than the younger more tender type, then tenderise it by mixing it with sliced kiwi fruit for an hour or so before cooking.

Serves 3–4

(DF) (LS) (LF)

Per serving (for 4): 180 cals | 6g fat 3g sat fat | 24g protein | 6g carbs 4.5g sugar | 1.3g salt

600g squid, trimmed (see page 20)
2 teaspoons coconut or light olive oil
2 garlic cloves, sliced
2–3 shallots, sliced
1 large green pepper, deseeded and cut into 2–3cm slices
½ teaspoon paprika
3 teaspoons fresh green peppercorns, or green or pink peppercorns in brine, rinsed and drained
4 spring onions, cut into 3cm pieces
1 ½ tablespoons oyster sauce
1–2 teaspoons fish sauce
5 tablespoons light coconut milk
1 tablespoon lime juice
1 heaped tablespoon chopped Thai basil
steamed rice, to serve

Cut the squid into 3 x 4cm strips and, using a sharp knife, score them in a crisscross pattern on the fleshy side. Heat the oil in a wok and add the garlic and shallots. Stir-fry for 1 minute, then add the squid and toss together over a high heat for 1 minute. Transfer to a bowl.

Add the green pepper to the wok and cook for 30 seconds. Sprinkle over the paprika, add the peppercorns and spring onions and toss together. Add the oyster sauce, fish sauce and coconut milk and return the squid, garlic and shallots to the wok. Toss together and taste for seasoning, then stir in the lime juice and Thai basil. Serve with steamed rice.

CHILLI CHICKEN STIR-FRY WITH BEANS & THAI BASIL

A super-quick, super-tasty and nutritious stir-fry perfect for a midweek supper. Thai basil has a more aniseed flavour than Italian basil, but if you can't find it, then use the smaller leaves of the latter. Basil has great superfood properties because it contains antibacterial, antimicrobial and anti-ageing properties and is high in antioxidants and flavenoids, which are cancer fighting. For a kids version, omit the chilli and if you prefer, use thigh meat instead of breast.

Serves 2

Per serving: 256 cals | 8g fat | 5g sat fat
40g protein | 7g carbs | 4g sugar | 1.8g salt

1 tablespoon coconut or light olive oil
3 garlic cloves, sliced
2 long red chillies, halved lengthways and widthways (deseed for less heat)
2 medium chicken breasts, sliced thinly against the grain
150g snake beans or green beans, trimmed and cut into 5cm lengths
½ onion, thinly sliced
5 tablespoons low-salt chicken stock
3 spring onions, cut into 5cm pieces
1 tablespoon oyster sauce
1 teaspoon reduced-salt soy sauce
1 teaspoon fish sauce
12 Thai basil leaves (see introduction)
ground white pepper
steamed rice or noodles, to serve

Heat the oil in a wok, add the garlic and chillies, and stir-fry for 1–2 minutes over a medium heat to soften them. Increase the heat, add the chicken and cook until browned all over. Add the beans and onion and stir-fry for 2 minutes.

Add the chicken stock and steam-fry the beans, preferably with a lid on, for 1 minute. Stir in the spring onions and oyster, soy and fish sauces. Fry for a final couple of minutes, then season with a pinch of white pepper. Turn off the heat, stir in the basil and serve immediately with rice or noodles.

STIR-FRIED CHICKEN WITH CASHEW NUTS

A favourite, instant stir-fry that is popular with all ages. Cashew nuts are really good for you as they contain heart-healthy monounsaturated fat, plus lots of antioxidants, magnesium and copper.

To keep stir-frying healthy, it's best to use a non-stick wok, as you'll need less oil. Also, try to get everything chopped and ready to go prior to cooking, so that you can be quick and orderly, preventing vegetables from being overcooked.

Shaoxing Chinese cooking wine, also known as Chinese rice wine, is sold in most supermarkets these days, and unlike normal white or red wine, will keep for months – it's a great store cupboard standby to add to stir-fries. However, if you can't find it, then dry sherry will do. You can also use 3–4 chicken breasts, instead of thighs, if you prefer.

Serves 4

PER SERVING: 422 cals | 20g fat | 6g sat fat 41g protein | 18g carbs | 9g sugar | 2.3g salt

600g boneless, skinless chicken thighs, fat removed, cut into chunks
2 teaspoons reduced-salt soy sauce
1 ½ tablespoons Shaoxing Chinese cooking wine or dry sherry
1 ½ tablespoons grated fresh ginger
1 large red chilli, deseeded and sliced (optional)
1 heaped tablespoon cornflour
2–3 teaspoons coconut or light olive oil
100g raw unsalted cashew nuts
2 small heads of broccoli, divided into florets
1 large red pepper, sliced
bunch of spring onions, cut into 4 cm pieces
125ml hot low-salt chicken stock or water
4 teaspoons fish sauce
1 tablespoon reduced-salt soy sauce
1 teaspoon clear honey, preferably raw
2 tablespoons oyster sauce
steamed rice or noodles, to serve

In a bowl mix together the chicken, soy sauce, wine or sherry, ginger, chilli (if using) and cornflour. Set aside to marinate for a few minutes.

Heat a wok over medium–high heat. Add the oil and when hot, add the cashew nuts and stir-fry until brown all over. Scoop them out using a slotted spoon and drain on kitchen paper.

Add the chicken and cook for 4–5 minutes, letting the meat sizzle and brown before turning it over – it will be three-quarters cooked through. Use the slotted spoon to transfer the meat to a bowl.

Add a little extra oil to the wok, if needed. When the oil is hot, add the broccoli and pepper and stir-fry for 2 minutes. Add the spring onions, stir-fry for 2–3 minutes, adding a little of the stock to steam the vegetables. Add the fish sauce, soy sauce, honey, oyster sauce and remaining stock. Return the chicken and nuts to the wok and stir over the heat for 1–2 minutes. Serve with rice or noodles.

SWEET & SOUR PORK

It's a favourite for many, but we all know that restaurant-made sweet and sour involves a lot of deep-frying and sugar, which isn't great. This version is packed with vegetables and uses fresh pineapple as opposed to the canned variety. For those who like a kick, adding the chilli will give you a bit of heat, but rather steers from the traditional version.

Serves 4–5

Per serving (for 5): 236 cals | 10g fat
4g sat fat | 20g protein | 15g carbs
11g sugar | 1.3g salt

400g pork fillet, cut against the grain into 1cm slices
1 tablespoon cornflour
2 teaspoons reduced-salt soy sauce
3 teaspoons coconut or light olive oil
1 tablespoon sesame oil
½ onion, cut into wedges
1 medium green or red pepper, cut into 3cm chunks
1 long red chilli (deseed for less heat), finely chopped (optional)
2 garlic cloves, sliced
300g fresh pineapple chunks
300ml hot chicken stock
½ cucumber, deseeded and cut into 2–3cm chunks
2 tomatoes, cut into 2–3cm chunks
1 ½ tablespoons oyster sauce
2 tablespoons low-salt and low-sugar tomato ketchup
ground white pepper
steamed rice, to serve

Put the pork fillet into a non-metallic bowl with the cornflour and soy sauce and stir together. Cover with clingfilm and marinate in the fridge for up to 4 hours.

Heat 2 teaspoons of the oil in a wok and add the pork. Stir-fry over a high heat until browned, then transfer to a bowl. Add the remaining teaspoon of oil and the sesame oil and stir-fry the onion, pepper and chilli (if using) over a medium heat for 2–3 minutes. Add the garlic and stir-fry for 1 minute before adding the pineapple and stock, and simmer over a medium heat for 10 minutes.

Add the cucumber, tomatoes, oyster sauce, ketchup and some white pepper and return the pork to the pan. Leave to bubble for 5 minutes, then taste, adding extra seasoning if required. Serve with rice.

JAPANESE BEEF RICE BOWL

A super-quick and very popular dish in both Japan and Korea, beef rice bowl, or gyudon, has many variations but is essentially quickly cooked beef and onions in a flavoured dashi stock on Japanese rice. This is traditionally served with a raw egg, to stir in when piping hot, and some shredded spring onion sprinkled on top. I prefer to add a bit of crunch and colour (as well as nutrition) and serve with soy beans, halved fine green beans or stir-fried Chinese greens. Another addition to the dish are mushrooms – enoki, shiitake or chestnut, if you like – quickly sautéed and set to one side before the beef is browned.

Traditional recipes for gyudon simmer both the beef and onions in dashi. My version seals the beef in a frying pan, then the simmered onions, dashi and remaining ingredients are added. It's as quick as the traditional version, but personally I prefer to brown the beef a little. In Asia we can buy packs of thinly sliced beef called shabu shabu (named after another similar Japanese recipe), but if you can't find it, use a super-sharp knife and cut the wafer-thin strips yourself. This is an occasion when I think brown rice adds so much to the recipe – I far prefer it to anything else.

Serves 2–3 (LGI) (GF) (DF) (LS)

PER SERVING (FOR 3): 212 cals | 12.5g fat
3g sat fat | 18g protein | 6g carbs
3.5g sugar | 0.2g salt

300ml Dashi Stock (see page 172) or light beef stock
1 large onion, sliced
2 teaspoons light olive oil
250g good-quality beef fillet or sirloin, trimmed and sliced wafer thin
2 tablespoons mirin
2 teaspoons sake, Shaoxing Chinese cooking wine or dry sherry
2 teaspoons tamari or reduced-salt soy sauce
3 spring onions, finely chopped
freshly ground black pepper
steamed brown rice, soya beans, green beans or
  stir-fried Chinese greens, to serve

Place the stock in a medium pan and bring up to a simmer. Add the onion, cover with a lid and simmer for 5 minutes until softened.

Meanwhile, heat the oil in a large frying pan, add the beef and, using chopsticks, separate it out so that it cooks evenly. Leave it to brown for 30 seconds or so before turning it over. Seal over a high heat, for a further 1–2 minutes.

Strain the onion, reserving the liquid, and add the onion to the frying pan with 150ml of the cooking stock, the mirin, the sake and the tamari or soy sauce (discard any remaining stock). Boil for 2 minutes, adding a grinding of black pepper. Turn off the heat, sprinkle with the spring onions and serve on a bed of brown rice with a selection of vegetables.

TERIYAKI BEEF STIR-FRY WITH MUSHROOMS & BABY CORN

To save time, you can use a shop-bought teriyaki marinade and add freshly grated ginger and garlic to it, as well as a teaspoon of sesame oil. However, to avoid potential added nasties, such as loads of sugar, sodium, additives and preservatives, make your own. It takes a couple of minutes from start to finish and tastes SO much better! This cries out for some cooked soba noodles to be mixed in at the end, but you could also serve it with steamed brown rice if you prefer. .

Serves 4

PER SERVING: 227 cals | 9g fat | 3g sat fat 22g protein | 15g carbs | 10.5g sugar 1.5g salt

For the teriyaki marinade
2 teaspoons grated fresh ginger
2 garlic cloves, finely chopped
1 ½ tablespoons clear honey, preferably raw
1 ½ teaspoons sesame oil
2 tablespoons tamari or reduced-salt soy sauce
2 ½ tablespoons mirin
1 long red chilli, with seeds, finely chopped
salt and freshly ground black pepper

For the stir-fry
350g beef fillet or trimmed sirloin, cut against the grain into thin slivers
2 teaspoons coconut or light olive oil
1 onion, sliced
8 shiitake or button mushrooms, quartered
150g baby corn, halved lengthways
6 water chestnuts, thickly sliced
200g Chinese or savoy cabbage, shredded
squeeze of lemon
noodles or steamed rice, to serve

Put all the marinade ingredients into a medium non-metallic bowl and whisk together. Add the beef and stir to coat. Cover and refrigerate for up to 2 hours or as long as you have got. Drain thoroughly in a sieve or colander placed over a bowl and reserve the drained marinade.

Heat half the oil in a large wok over a high heat until smoking hot and add the beef. Cook the beef in two batches if the wok is small – this will avoid it steam-cooking and not gaining good colour. Leave the beef to sizzle and brown on one side, before turning it over – this will give the stir-fry a good flavour. Once browned, transfer to a bowl using a slotted spoon.

Add the remaining oil and sauté the onion for 1–2 minutes, stirring it in the wok. Add the mushrooms and stir-fry over a high heat for a further 2 minutes. Add the baby corn, water chestnuts and 3 tablespoons of cold water and toss the vegetables together for 2–3 minutes. Return the beef to the pan with the cabbage, the reserved marinade, a pinch of salt and a squeeze of lemon. Stir-fry for 1 minute, taste for seasoning and serve with cooked noodles or steamed rice.

Curries

We are big curry fans in our house, both Indian and South-East Asian. Midweek for two or for a large group of friends at the weekend, they perk up any occasion and have the great advantage of tasting better when made ahead of time. One of my earliest memories of curry as a child was my stepmother's camping curry, made with lamb and a canned curry sauce, which, though it sounds pretty rank on paper, was the highlight of an otherwise fairly miserable time spent in a leaking tent, shared with my brothers Simon and Al!

In the 1980s, the influence of Asian flavours still hadn't really hit us in England, and it was jarred Indian curry pastes that we all turned too for a taste of the exotic – or a takeaway from one of the many curry houses that we had to choose from locally. My first South East Asian curry was, unsurprisingly, a Thai green chicken curry – though I'm pleased to say it was eaten in Thailand, in the early 1990s. Baby aubergines, peas and the most delectable mild coconut sauce to pour over fragrant rice were a joy to behold and by the time I returned to England, Thai restaurants were popping up in London. Supermarkets cotton on to these things quickly and there was suddenly the chance to cook with new and exciting ingredients at home – lemongrass, kaffir lime leaves and coconut milk featuring in a new type of curry – which offered something lighter and more fragrant.

Thai, laksa and massaman pastes are all readily available in most supermarkets, but I urge you to make your own on a rainy day and keep them in the freezer. The taste difference is enormous and, needless to say, the salt content and additives of these pastes are significant too. Much better to make your own in a batch and just use them when needed.

QUICK VEGETABLE CURRY

Apart from the fresh ginger, which I keep in my freezer, and the garlic, which I always have lurking in my fridge, I've tried to keep this curry paste quite storecupboardy, so you can rustle it up on a midweek night.

As with all curries, the veg you put in it is totally adaptable, so feel free to substitute okra for courgette or throw in some pumpkin or extra peppers if you don't have quite enough of something. This is a fairly mild curry, so you can up the chilli flakes if you like. You can also add some chickpeas, new potatoes or indeed some chicken if you want to satisfy a hungrier guest. One tip – make it the day before you want to eat it – it will taste even better!

For a lower-fat version, use coconut milk instead of coconut cream.

Serves 2–3

(V) (VE) (LG) (GF) (LS)

PER SERVING (FOR 3): 190 cals | 10.5g fat
7.5g sat fat | 5.5g protein | 17g carbs
15g sugar | 0.1g salt

For the spice paste
6cm piece fresh ginger, peeled and grated
3 garlic cloves, roughly chopped
2–3 generous pinches of dried chilli flakes
1 teaspoon cumin seeds
1 teaspoon ground turmeric
5 cardamom pods, crushed and seeds reserved (pods discarded)

For the curry
2–4 teaspoons coconut or light olive oil
1 large aubergine, cut into 5cm chunks
1 large or 2 small onions, sliced
1 large red pepper, cut into 5cm chunks
150g small cauliflower florets
4 large ripe tomatoes, roughly chopped
150g cherry tomatoes
1 tablespoon chopped coriander
squeeze of lime
2 tablespoons coconut cream or light coonut milk
salt and freshly ground black pepper
fragrant rice, to serve

Put all the spice paste ingredients into a pestle and mortar or mini blender and simply pound or whizz all the ingredients together to form a rough paste.

Heat 2 teaspoons of the oil in a wok and add the aubergine. Brown all over and then transfer to a plate. (You may need to add a little more oil at this point.) Add the onions to the pan and sauté over a low heat until they have softened. Then add the pepper and stir-fry for a couple of minutes. Spoon in the spice paste and cook for 2–3 minutes, stirring constantly. Next add the cauliflower, tomatoes and the browned aubergine. Pour in enough hot water to come just below the surface of the vegetables. Season and simmer for 8–10 minutes or until the vegetables are tender.

Just before serving, stir in the coriander, add a squeeze of lime and drizzle with the coconut cream. Serve with fragrant rice.

THAI SWEET POTATO & SPINACH CURRY

A great accompaniment to other dishes or a veggie main course. For a non-veggie version, add 2–3 skinless chicken breasts cut into chunks to the sauce at the same time as the sweet potato.

Serves 4

Per serving: 268 cals | 13g fat | 8g sat fat 7.5g protein | 31g carbs | 11g sugar | 2.1g salt

2 teaspoons coconut or light olive oil
1 medium red onion, sliced
4 tablespoons Thai Red Curry Paste (see page 174)
400ml hot chicken or vegetable stock
400ml can light coconut milk
4 sweet potatoes (about 500g), peeled and cut into 5cm chunks
125g canned bamboo shoots (drained weight), sliced into 5mm strips
5 large fresh kaffir lime leaves (or 9–10 dried), shredded
150g Chinese leaves or baby spinach
handful of Thai basil leaves
handful of coriander leaves
juice of 1 lime
1 ½ tablespoons fish sauce
ground white pepper

Heat the oil in a wok or large pan and add the onion. Stir-fry for 5 minutes over a medium heat, then add the curry paste. Stir and let the paste sizzle over the heat for a minute or two, then add the stock and coconut milk. Bring up to a simmer, then add the sweet potatoes, bamboo shoots, kaffir lime leaves and some ground white pepper and cook for a further 20 minutes or until the sweet potato is just tender.

Stir in the Chinese leaves or spinach and nearly all the herbs, the lime juice and fish sauce and serve the curry garnished with the remaining herbs.

CURRIES

THAI RED CURRY WITH PRAWNS, PUMPKIN & MANGO

I find it's tricky to give people a quantity of paste to use, as everyone's taste is so different. I suggest that if you like curry with a bit of a kick, start off with 3 tablespoons – you can always fry a little more paste later and add it to the curry in the pan if you feel it's not quite hitting the mark. This is also a great curry for children – just use 1¹/2 tablespoons of paste instead of the full amount. If you don't have time to make the paste or don't have any in the freezer, I reluctantly suggest that you could use store-bought, but do go for a decent-quality variety with a healthy-looking ingredients list.

If you are watching the calories, then use light coconut milk, however, coconut milk contains 'good fat', is full of nutrients (it contains lauric acid, which is said to help protect the body from infections and viruses) and is lactose-free and also recommended for those following the Paleo diet, so though it does contain fat it's okay to use in moderation.

Serves 4-6

(LGI) (GF) (DF) (LS) (LF)

Per serving (for 6): 184 cals | 7g fat
4.5g sat fat | 15g protein | 14g carbs
13g sugar | 1.6g salt

3-4 tablespoons Thai Red Curry Paste (see page 174)
400ml can coconut milk or light coconut milk (see introduction)
300ml hot low-salt chicken stock
700g pumpkin or butternut squash (unprepared weight), peeled and cut into 3-4cm chunks
400g medium raw prawns, peeled and deveined, tails left on (800g unpeeled weight)
1 large, firm mango (about 450g) peeled, stoned and cut into 3-4cm chunks
good squeeze of lime
2 tablespoons fish sauce
generous handful of chopped coriander leaves
8 Thai or sweet basil leaves, chopped
fragrant rice, to serve

Heat a wok and add the curry paste, stir-fry for 2 minutes, then add the coconut milk and stock and bring up to a simmer. Add the pumpkin or butternut and cook for 10 minutes or until three-quarters cooked.

Add the prawns and cook for 3-4 minutes, stirring occasionally. Add the mango, lime juice, half the fish sauce, half of the coriander and all the basil and stir together. Taste, adding extra fish sauce or lime as needed. Garnish with the remaining coriander and serve with fragrant rice.

Tip: Use cubed chicken thighs instead of the prawns, brown the meat when you fry the paste at the start and continue as above.

EAST MEETS WEST LAKSA

The reason for the name is that, in order to create an authentic Malay Laksa, you need ingredients such as candlenut and laksa leaves, which are going to be pretty hard to find in some parts of the world. So, this version is as near as I can get, without resorting to a shop-bought paste.

Laksa is one of those recipes that is made slightly differently in every country from Malaysia to Brunei to Indonesia and Singapore; they all have their own version of this main-course soup. Some contain tamarind for a hot-and-sour flavour and some, like this, are coconut based. All of them are delicious in their own way. If you don't have a favourite curry powder, an Indian medium-strength curry powder is fine.

Serves 4 (DF)(LS)

PER SERVING: 465 cals | 23g fat | 11g sat fat 43g protein | 21g carbs | 3g sugar | 2.9g salt

Veggie Laksa: Make per the recipe, but use vegetable stock and omit the seafood and fish sauce. Add 100g of fine green beans, trimmed and halved, to the pan for the final 3 minutes of cooking and a head of pak choi, stems chopped into 5cm pieces and leaves halved, for the final minute. Fried tofu can also be added. Top the soup bowls with 2 freshly cooked and quartered hard-boiled eggs.

12 large raw prawns, unpeeled
4 teaspoons coconut or light olive oil
650ml hot chicken or vegetable stock
4 heaped tablespoons Laksa Paste (see page 176)
1 teaspoon ground turmeric
1 teaspoon curry powder
4 stems of laksa leaves, leaves removed and stems discarded, or the stems of a bunch of coriander, finely chopped
400ml can coconut milk or light coconut milk
500g squid, prepared (see page 20) cut into 7.5cm pieces, then scored
150g medium noodles or rice vermicelli, or 200g flat noodles
100g beansprouts
juice of 1 lime
fish sauce, to taste
1 heaped tablespoon chopped mint leaves
2 tablespoons chopped coriander leaves
2 freshly cooked hard-boiled eggs, quartered, to garnish (optional)

Peel and devein the prawns, reserving the heads and shells. Heat 1 teaspoon of the oil in a large non-stick pan, add the heads and shells and stir-fry for a couple of minutes until they are crisp and golden. Add the stock, bring to the boil and leave to simmer, covered, for 5 minutes. Then strain through a sieve and discard the heads and shells.

Heat 2 teaspoons of the oil in the same pan, and stir-fry the paste for 5 minutes over a low heat. Then add the turmeric and curry powder and stir for a further minute. Add the laksa leaves or chopped coriander stems, then pour in the coconut milk. Bring up to a simmer and cook gently for 10 minutes.

Meanwhile, heat a frying pan or wok with 1 teaspoon of the oil and stir-fry the squid and prawns over a high heat for 1–2 minutes.

Cook the noodles according to the packet instructions, drain and divide between 4 warmed bowls.

Add the cooked seafood and any juices to the laksa pan along with the beansprouts and cook for 1 minute. Add the lime juice and fish sauce to taste.

Ladle the laksa over the noodles, trying to divide the prawns and squid pieces equally between the bowls. Sprinkle with the chopped herbs and serve garnished with hard-boiled eggs, if you like.

CURRIES

RAINBOW FISH CURRY

Traditional fish head curry is sold everywhere in Singapore, and this is my nod to it. A delicious, colourful and super-healthy curry using chunks of fish, loads of veg and pineapple. Like so many dishes eaten in Singapore there are many variations, influenced by the Indian, Malay and Chinese families living here – many using a pre-made fish curry powder, but as this quite hard to locate elsewhere, I suggest using a regular medium curry powder instead. Use a firm white fish such as tilapia (cream snapper), snapper, cod, coley or pollack as you don't want it to break up too much during cooking. The thinner the fish fillet, the less cooking required. If you can, ask at the fish counter for some fish bones. To make a quick fish stock, simply pop them into a pan with about 600ml of boiling water and simmer gently whilst frying the onions. If this isn't possible, water will be fine.

I like to make the curry sauce earlier in the day and then leave it to mellow and soften a little before reheating, adding the fish and coconut milk just before serving.

Serves 6

Per serving: 202 cals | 4g fat | 2.5g sat fat 28g protein | 13g carbs | 12g sugar 0.3g salt

1 tablespoon coconut or light olive oil
75g shallots or red onion, chopped
½ teaspoon yellow mustard seeds
4 garlic cloves, chopped
1 tablespoon grated fresh ginger
1 ½ teaspoons medium curry powder
1 ½ teaspoons ground turmeric
½ teaspoon dried chilli flakes
3 lemongrass stalks, tough outer leaves removed and remaining inner stalks bashed with a rolling pin
2 long green chillies, halved lengthways with seeds
15 curry leaves
500ml hot fish stock or water (see introduction)
10 okra, trimmed and halved crossways
1 red pepper, cut into 5cm chunks
200g aubergine, cut into 5cm chunks
3 tomatoes, cut into wedges
½ small pineapple, peeled, cored and cut into chunks (about 250g)
2 teaspoons grated palm sugar or clear honey, or a sprinkling of stevia
2 tablespoons tamarind paste or purée (see Tip on page 92)
½ heaped teaspoon flaked sea salt
850g skinned and boned meaty fish (total weight with bones about 1kg), cut into 5-6cm cubes (reserve the bones)
4 tablespoons light coconut milk
brown rice, to serve

Heat the oil in a large wok or saucepan and fry the shallots or onion gently for 6-8 minutes or until soft. Add the mustard seeds, garlic and ginger for the final 3 minutes.

Mix the spices and chilli flakes in a small bowl with 2 tablespoons of cold water. Add to the onion, along with the lemongrass, green chillies and curry leaves and fry for 2 minutes, stirring all the time to make sure the spices are cooked. Pour in the fish stock or water. Stir once and bring up to the boil, then cover and simmer for 5 minutes.

Stir in the okra, pepper, aubergine, tomatoes, pineapple, palm sugar, tamarind and salt and cook, covered, for a further 6-7 minutes or until the aubergine is nearly tender. Finally, add the fish and coconut milk, making sure the fish is submerged in the liquid, and simmer gently, covered, for a final 5 minutes or until the fish is just cooked, stirring once. Serve with brown rice.

CURRIES

VIETNAMESE FRAGRANT GREEN CHICKEN CURRY

Having a stash of ready-made paste in the freezer is an absolute lifesaver at times when you want a healthy quick fix and an alternative to the usual soups or Bolognese sauce. However, if you don't have time to make some, then use a ready-made Thai green curry paste, but do check the ingredients list for any nasties. Add some extra lime zest, shredded lime leaves and turmeric to it, plus plenty of herbs and lime juice at the end.

Vietnamese curries are to me even fresher, zestier and aromatic than the more familiar Thai green curries we all know and love. The addition of superfood turmeric is great too – as it is proven to have numerous healing properties. Vietnamese curries often have added cubed potato, sweet potato or pumpkin, which you can add at the start of cooking, if you like.

Serves 3–4

Per serving (for 4): 281 cals | 11g fat 8g sat fat | 39g protein | 7g carbs 6g sugar | 1.8g salt

½ quantity Vietnamese Fragrant Green Curry Paste (see page 177)
8 boned chicken thighs, skinned, or 4 large chicken breasts, cut into chunks
1 red pepper, deseeded and cut into 4cm chunks
6 spring onions, trimmed and cut into 4cm pieces
400ml can coconut milk or light coconut milk
125ml hot chicken stock
250g prepared mixed vegetables, such as okra, green beans, mangetout, sugar snap peas, asparagus or water chestnuts (peeled and halved), larger vegetables cut into 4–5cm pieces
20 Thai basil leaves or 10 sweet basil leaves, torn
2 heaped tablespoons chopped coriander leaves
2 tablespoons fish sauce
generous squeeze of lime juice
sea salt
Thai jasmine rice, to serve

In a large non-stick pan or wok, stir-fry the paste over a gentle heat for 3–4 minutes. Add the chicken, pepper, spring onions and a sprinkling of salt and fry for a further 5 minutes.

Add half the coconut milk and simmer for 5–6 minutes, before adding the remaining coconut milk and stock, bringing back up to a simmer and cooking for 3–4 minutes.

As the curry simmers, add the vegetables in order of cooking time (cook okra, water chestnuts and green beans for 3–4 minutes; mangetout, sugar snaps or asparagus for the last 30 seconds or so). Once the vegetables are cooked, add most of the basil and coriander, along with the fish sauce and lime juice. Stir and taste, adding extra fish sauce or lime juice if needed. Serve garnished with the remaining herbs and with some Thai jasmine rice.

MASSAMAN CHICKEN TRAY BAKE

Muslim in origin, the roots of massaman curry are somewhat disputed – some say it is from central Thailand whilst others from the southern part of the country. It is mild but aromatic in flavour, with the warmer spices of clove, cinnamon and cardamom being combined with coconut rather than the more fragrant herbs and spices found in a green curry, for example. It is often made using beef or, in this version, chicken pieces. Sweet potatoes would also work well.

Serves 6

Per serving: 343 cals | 14g fat | 7g sat fat 36g protein | 18g carbs | 6g sugar | 1.5g salt

12 bone-in chicken thighs, skinned
125g small whole shallots
5 cardamom pods, split
3 tablespoons Massaman Curry Paste (see page 177)
1 tablespoon coconut or light olive oil
1 tablespoon tamarind paste or purée (see Tip on page 92)
1 teaspoon palm sugar, grated
200ml hot chicken stock
400ml can light coconut milk
3 medium potatoes (about 400g), cut into 2.5cm chunks (optional)
150g sugar snap peas, destrung, or green beans, trimmed and halved
2 tablespoons fish sauce
good squeeze of lime
1 tablespoon roasted whole peanuts or cashew nuts
handful of coriander leaves, chopped

Preheat the oven to 200°C/gas mark 6.

In a non-metallic bowl, mix the chicken, shallots and cardamom pods with the curry paste and oil and leave to marinate for 20 minutes. Transfer the chicken and shallots, along with any paste, to a wide casserole dish or deep roasting tin – spreading the chicken out as much as possible. Roast for 20 minutes.

Meanwhile, mix together the tamarind purée, sugar, stock and coconut milk in a small pan. Heat until simmering, then add it to the casserole or roasting tin along with the potatoes (if using). Stir everything together and cover with a lid or foil. Reduce the oven temperature to 180°C/gas mark 4 and cook for a further 45-60 minutes or until the potatoes and chicken are cooked, stirring halfway through.

Steam the sugar snap peas or green beans for 2-3 minutes, then stir into the curry along with the fish sauce and lime juice. Sprinkle with the nuts and coriander leaves and serve immediately.

BURMESE CHICKEN & POTATO CURRY

It is a wonder to me that wherever a country is placed, its cuisine will reflect the countries that it borders, and nothing could be truer than in Burma/Myanmar. There's the usual typically Asian combination of salty, sweet, hot and sour, but as you will see in this recipe, also the subtle addition of Indian flavours too.

All Burmese curries seem to have the same basic paste to begin, which handily freezes extremely well, so you can make large batches and just defrost it as needed. Traditionally, the curries would contain a lot more oil and sometimes the addition of coconut, but I have kept this version fresh and healthy. Try it with cubed pork shoulder too – cover and cook it until nearly tender, before adding the potatoes and beans as per the recipe.

Serves 4–6

Per serving (for 6): 340 cals | 11g fat
5g sat fat | 48g protein | 14g carbs
5g sugar | 1.8g salt

1 ½ teaspoons ground turmeric
1 ½ teaspoons curry powder
1 ½ teaspoons garam masala
1.25kg boned chicken thighs (10–12), skinned
½ quantity Burmese Curry Paste (see page 176)
250ml hot chicken stock or water
1 large lemongrass stalk, tough outer leaves removed and remaining inner stalk very finely chopped
¾ teaspoon palm sugar or clear honey, preferably raw
5 ripe plum tomatoes, chopped
6 new potatoes, halved or quartered into bite-sized pieces
150g fine green beans, trimmed
2 tablespoons fish sauce
good squeeze of lime
chopped coriander and chopped shallots, to garnish
brown rice, to serve

Mix the turmeric, curry powder and garam masala with a little cold water to make a paste. Place the chicken in a non-metallic dish, spoon the paste over and toss to thoroughly coat each thigh. Cover and refrigerate for 10 minutes to 4 hours.

Heat the curry paste in a large non-stick saucepan or wok and add the chicken. Stir over a medium heat for 3 minutes to seal the chicken. Add the stock or water and the lemongrass, bring back up to the boil and simmer for 15 minutes, stirring every so often.

Add the palm sugar or honey and tomatoes. Cook for a further 25 minutes, then add the potatoes, bring to the boil again and cook over a low-medium heat for a further 10 minutes. Add the green beans and continue to cook for about 5 minutes or until the potatoes are just tender. Add the fish sauce and lime juice, taste for seasoning, adding a little more if needed, and top with the coriander and shallots. Serve with brown rice.

LIGHTER BEEF RENDANG

There is a wonderful Peranakan restaurant near me called Violet Oon's, owned by the Singaporean celebrity chef of the same name. Though it dabbles a little with some fusion dishes I think it particularly excels at the traditional recipes such as the slow-cooked beef rendang. It has a thick, coconut gravy, which just coats the meat, and the beef is melt-in-the-mouth tender.

The key to enjoying this very rich curry is to serve it in small bowls, with some rice on the side and some glorious colourful pickled vegetables to add crunch and well-needed sharpness. A coconut beef curry is sadly never going to be low calorie, but this version is certainly lighter than most and the richness of this curry means a little goes a long way!

Serves 6

PER SERVING: 451 cals | 28g fat | 16g sat fat
41g protein | 8g carbs | 7g sugar | 0.3g salt

For the spice paste

6 dried long red chillies or cascabel dried chillies
6cm piece of galangal or ginger, or a mix of both, peeled and chopped
4 fat garlic cloves, chopped
125g shallots, roughly chopped
4 lemongrass stalks, tough outer leaves removed and remaining inner stalks sliced

For the curry

1kg shin of beef, trimmed and cut into 4cm pieces
spray oil
½ teaspoon ground cloves
¾ teaspoon ground turmeric
2 cinnamon sticks
8 cardamom pods, bashed lightly with a rolling pin
350ml hot well-flavoured beef stock
400ml can light coconut milk
3 fresh kaffir lime leaves (or 5 dried), shredded
2 tablespoons tamarind paste or purée (see Tip on page 92)
1 heaped teaspoon grated palm sugar
1 heaped tablespoon desiccated coconut
1 teaspoon flaked sea salt
rice and Pickled Vegetables (see page 179), to serve

To make the paste, soak the chillies in 100ml of boiling water for 20 minutes, then drain and put into a mini processor or pestle and mortar with all the other paste ingredients, plus 4 tablespoons of cold water. Blitz or pound to form a coarse paste. Transfer the paste to a large non-metallic bowl, add the beef and stir to coat. Set aside.

Preheat the oven to 150°C/gas mark 2.

Spray a large heavy-based flameproof casserole with some oil and heat. Add the beef and stir over a high heat for about 4 minutes to cook the paste and start to seal the beef. Add the cloves, turmeric, cinnamon sticks and cardamom pods. Stir for 30 seconds before pouring in the beef stock and coconut milk. Add the lime leaves, tamarind purée, palm sugar, desiccated coconut and salt, stir well and bring up to a simmer. Cover and cook in the oven for 2 hours or until the beef is tender, removing the lid after 1 hour. Serve with rice and pickled vegetables.

Baked, BBQ & One Pot

Asians are the kings when it comes to stocks, marinades, tasty sauces and glazes as far as I am concerned, and this chapter shows you how you can make the most of these richly flavoured recipes without eating unhealthily. The key is to be aware of what you are adding – condiments and shop-bought sauces often have very high amounts of additives, MSG, preservatives and salt, so the key is to use lots of spices and fresh aromatics, and when you are marinating or adding a sauce, to make your own. It's just as quick, so long as you have a few key ingredients to hand. Star anise, five spice powder, garlic, chilli, miso, mirin and ginger are just a few of the wonderful flavours to add to the pot as healthy alternatives. And there is also a place for soy sauce – but use the low-salt varieties and opt for raw honey or stevia over white sugar when adding sweetness to marinades.

Quite a few recipes in this chapter make use of larger cuts – pork fillet, whole snapper, roast duck and whole chicken, for example. There are also some slow-cooked braises and some great ways to barbecue. And the good news is the recipes are simple and tasty enough to keep everyone in the family happy and they're all nutritious and healthy too.

STEAM-BAKED SALMON & VEGETABLE PARCELS WITH ASIAN DRESSING

Super quick and easy, this dish is equally suitable for a midweek supper or dinner for friends. Sea bass or tilapia (cream snapper) fillets will also work as well – just adjust the cooking time according to thickness. Prepare the parcels and dressing earlier in the day and keep them in the fridge, but pour over the dressing just before sealing the parcels and cooking. If they have been in the fridge for more than half an hour, give them an extra 5 minutes or so in the oven. If you are not a fan of ginger, you can use lime slices to top the fish.

Serves 4

PER SERVING: 331 cals | 18.5g fat | 3g sat fat 34g protein | 7g carbs | 5g sugar | 1.2g salt

For the dressing

1 heaped teaspoon grated fresh ginger
3 tablespoons reduced-salt soy sauce
1 teaspoon balsamic vinegar
1 tablespoon clear honey, preferably raw
1 ½ teaspoons sesame oil
1 long red chilli, deseeded and chopped
3 spring onions, trimmed and finely chopped
juice of 1 ½ limes

For the parcels

4 x 150g salmon fillets, skinned
400g quick-cook prepared mixed vegetables, such as halved baby corn, mangetout, sugar snap peas, small broccoli florets, pak choi, pepper pieces or thinly sliced carrots
coriander leaves, to garnish
steamed brown rice, to serve

Preheat the oven to 200°C/gas mark 6.

Cut 4 pieces of foil large enough to each hold a salmon piece and some vegetables and to scrunch into loose-fitting parcels.

Make the dressing by combining all the ingredients in a jug.

Place one-quarter of the vegetables in the centre of each piece of foil and place the fish on top. Divide the dressing equally between the parcels. Scrunch the foil to make loose, sealed parcels, so that the vapour inside will have room to steam the fish. Place the parcels on a baking tray. Place onto the middle shelf and cook the fish for 15–20 minutes, depending on thickness, or until the fish is cooked through. It's important not to overcook the fish as it will be dry. Use the tip of a knife to carefully check for doneness – it should look moist but not raw and pull apart easily.

Transfer the fish and vegetables onto serving plates and pour over the sauce. Serve with steamed brown rice.

BAKED RED SNAPPER WITH LEMONGRASS & GINGER

This is such a tasty treat and looks wonderful too. Depending on availability or what you prefer, you can make this recipe using 4 smaller fish instead. Just reduce the cooking time according to their size and check carefully to make sure they aren't overcooked.

To get ahead, you can make the dressing earlier in the day and just keep it covered in the fridge. Use half or one chilli, with seeds or without – the choice is yours depending on whether you want extra heat. Get the fish parcels ready to go, then pour over the marinade just before you want to cook.

Serves 4

(LGI) (GF) (DF) (LS) (LF)

PER SERVING: 262 cals | 5g fat | 1g sat fat
50g protein | 5g carbs | 5g sugar | 1.1g salt

2 x 500–700g whole snapper, or 4 x 200–300g whole red snapper or sea bream, descaled and cleaned
4 garlic cloves, finely chopped
2 heaped tablespoons grated fresh ginger
juice of 1 lime
1 ½ tablespoons reduced-salt or light soy sauce
½–1 long red chilli, depending on heat required, deseeded, and chopped
1 tablespoon clear honey, preferably raw
1 ½ tablespoons fish sauce
2 teaspoons sesame oil
4 spring onions, trimmed, stems and tops chopped
2 lemongrass stalks, tough outer leaves removed and remaining inner stalks very finely chopped
small bunch of coriander, stems and leaves roughly chopped
steamed rice, to serve

Preheat the oven to 220°C/gas mark 7. Line a large roasting dish with foil, so that it comes over the sides of the dish.

Make 3 slashes on top of each fish, one-third of the way down.

In a bowl, mix together the garlic, ginger, lime juice, soy sauce, chilli, honey, fish sauce and sesame oil.

Mix together the spring onions and lemongrass and sprinkle three-quarters over the foil. Place the slashed fish on top and stuff them with the remaining spring onion mixture.

Pour over the ginger and garlic mixture, rubbing it into each cut, then scatter over the coriander. Top the fish with another sheet of foil and then scrunch the foil together to make a large parcel.

Bake the large fish for 25–35 minutes and the smaller fish 20–25 minutes or until they are cooked through, the flesh is opaque and easily comes away from the bones. Transfer onto individual plates or a large platter, drizzle with the cooking juices and serve with steamed rice.

BAKED, BBQ & ONE POT

MISO COD

This recipe uses white miso, which is slightly sweeter and less salty than the red variety. You can use red miso, but you should reduce the quantity by one-third. Any white fish fillets will work well in this recipe and mackerel also marries well with miso, so feel free to use fresh mackerel fillets as an alternative. The fish needs to be marinated for at least 24 hours, so you need to prepare it a day or so in advance.

I like to serve the fish with steamed basmati or brown basmati rice, some delicately stir-fried greens such as pak choi or the Sweet & Sour Cucumber Salad on page 54.

Serves 4

Per serving: 223 cals | 2g fat | 0.5g sat fat 34g protein | 13g carbs | 7g sugar | 1.3g salt

3 tablespoons white miso paste
2 teaspoons clear honey, preferably raw
100ml sake, Shaoxing Chinese cooking wine or white wine
3 tablespoons mirin
1 tablespoon grated fresh ginger
4 x 200g thick pieces of very fresh cod fillet or other white fish, skin on
steamed rice and stir-fried greens or salad, to serve

Combine the miso paste, honey, sake or wine, mirin and ginger together in a small saucepan. Bring the marinade to the boil, then simmer for 3–4 minutes until it has reduced by about half and thickened slightly. Pour the marinade into a shallow, non-metallic dish, large enough to hold the fish in a single layer and leave it to cool completely.

Wash the cod pieces and pat them dry with kitchen paper. Place the cod in the cold marinade and liberally coat the fish with the marinade. Cover with clingfilm and refrigerate for 24–48 hours.

Preheat the grill to high. Lightly wipe off any excess marinade from the fish. Place the cod in an ovenproof dish, skin-side up, and grill for 4–6 minutes until the cod begins to blacken. Turn over and grill for another 4 minutes. The fish should flake into large pieces if lightly pushed and should be opaque all the way through.

Serve with steamed rice and stir-fried greens or Sweet & Sour Cucumber Salad.

AROMATIC POACHED CHICKEN & BROTH

This is another make-grandma-proud moment, as I work out the numerous suppers and lunches I can get from this poached chicken and its tasty stock. Not only is this dish economical, it's also really healthy and easy to make. You can include the meat in so many dishes – as well as fried rice or noodles, serve it with ginger-spiked rice (simply cook the rice with 4–5 slices of ginger) and Asian steamed veg, or use it for the Chicken, Mango & Rice Salad (see page 88) or Vietnamese-style Chicken Salad (see page 66) as well as numerous other recipes. The broth can be used to make a whole host of soups: classic and comforting: Chicken & Sweetcorn Soup (see page 45), Vietnamese Pho (see page 48), Healing 10-Minute Noodles in Broth (see page 46) and Spicy Roasted Pumpkin, Coconut & Peanut Soup (see page 38).

Makes approximately 1.6 litres stock and cooked chicken for 4–6 servings

(LGI) (GF) (DF) (LS) (LF)

PER SERVING (FOR 6): 164 cals | 3g fat 0.8g sat fat | 30g protein | 4g carbs 3g sugar | 0.9g salt

1.25–1.5 kg whole chicken
2 celery sticks, cut into 3
2 carrots, quartered
4 spring onions, halved, or 1 onion, quartered
8cm piece of fresh ginger, left unpeeled and thinly sliced
6 garlic cloves, squashed with the blade of a knife
3 star anise
1 red chilli, split lengthways, or ½ teaspoon dried chilli flakes (optional)
small bunch of coriander, stems and leaves chopped (optional)
½ teaspoon black peppercorns
2 bay leaves
2 ½ tablespoons reduced-salt soy sauce
1.25–1.5 kg whole chicken

Season the chicken inside the cavity and all over, then put into a large pan with all the other ingredients and 2.75 litres of cold water, making sure that the chicken is completely covered in liquid (top up if need be). Bring up to a simmer over a medium to high heat, then cover and slowly cook, just bubbling gently for 30 minutes, turning over once in the stock.

Turn off the heat, remove the lid and leave the chicken in the cooking liquid for a further 30 minutes, before taking it out. Either remove the meat from the chicken and eat with the broth immediately or set aside and cool then chill until ready to use. Strain the stock, reserve the vegetables and chill or freeze the broth for later use too. (You can serve the vegetables with the chicken and rice or discard.)

Poaching chicken breasts: If you prefer to poach chicken breasts instead of a whole bird, simply halve the quantity of ingredients for the stock (omit the soy sauce) and once it's simmered for 20 minutes, submerge 4 small chicken breasts (at room temperature) in the boiling stock, cover, take off the heat and leave for 20 minutes before removing using a slotted spoon. Use this light stock to add to stews or soups.

Light-flavoured stock: If you just want to make a good light-flavoured Asian chicken stock without cooking any meat, use 2 leftover roast chicken carcasses or 500g of chicken wings – just follow the recipe above, but simmer for 1½ hours and strain – there's no need to rest off the heat.

CRISPY PANKO BAKED CHICKEN GOUJONS

Crispy chicken in breadcrumbs is a great favourite with all ages in our house. They are useful to have in the freezer too. Simply prepare a batch and freeze them ready to bake or fry. Panko crumbs are easy to find and are a great storecupboard alternative to homemade breadcrumbs. They are also fabulous as a coating on fish and prawns too. Baking the goujons helps keep them healthy.

Serve with Rainbow Slaw (see page 58), the Soba Noodle & Edamame Salad (see page 72) or the Watercress, Asian Pear & Mint Salad (see page 60).

Makes approximately 20 goujons

(LG) (DF) (LS) (LF)

PER GOUJON: 71 cals | 2g fat | 0.5g sat fat
8.5g protein | 5.5g carbs | 0.7g sugar
0.3g salt

4 large chicken breasts
2 tablespoons tamari or reduced-salt soy sauce
2 teaspoons clear honey, preferably raw
spray oil
50–70g cornflour
2 free-range medium eggs
75g panko crumbs
salad, mashed potatoes or Healthy Fried Rice (see page 77), to serve
freshly ground black pepper

Sandwich the chicken breasts between clingfilm and bash on a chopping board using a rolling pin until they are of an equal thickness – just enough to even them out a bit, but not too thin or they will dry out. Cut the chicken breasts against the grain into thickish strips of a similar size (around 5 or 6 strips per breast). Place the chicken strips in a non-metallic shallow dish along with 1 tablespoon of the tamari or soy sauce and the honey, cover and marinate in the fridge for 20 minutes to 1 hour.

Preheat the oven to 190°C/gas mark 5. Line a baking tray with baking parchment and spray it with oil.

Sprinkle half the cornflour onto a plate and beat the eggs in a shallow bowl with some black pepper and the remaining soy sauce. Place the panko crumbs in a separate shallow bowl.

Dip the chicken strips first into the cornflour, then dust off and dip into the beaten egg, then coat in the crumbs. Replace the cornflour on the plate with the remainder half way through (it will get sticky). Place the coated chicken strips onto the lined tray and spray them all over with oil. Bake for 20–30 minutes or until golden and cooked through, turning once and spraying again if they look too dry. Serve with salad or Healthy Fried Rice.

BAKED, BBQ & ONE POT

FIVE SPICE ROAST DUCK

This is never going to be a low-calorie option, but I believe in allowing an indulgence once in a while, and this method of roasting the birds on a rack is a much healthier option than some recipes. It's a good idea to get into the habit of making the portions smaller with rich meats and to serve them with plenty of vegetables and rice.

Roasting two ducks may seem like a hassle, but you will probably find they'll fit side by side on a roasting rack. It's always such a pleasure to find leftover duck meat in the fridge too, as you then have a great reason to make Fresh Duck, Spring Onion & Hoisin Rolls (see page 32) or Healthy Fried Rice (see page 77) with added leftover shredded duck the next day. Make a batch of the plum sauce in advance and keep it in the fridge for up to a week or pop it in the freezer.

However, you can of course use duck breasts, if you wish. Season with five spice, salt and pepper, then cook the scored breasts skin-side down in a griddle pan, pouring away any fat as you go, for 12–15 minutes, then turn over and cook for 4–5 minutes on the other side. Rest, then remove the fat before serving sliced.

Serves 6–8

Per portion (for 8): 495 cals | 29g fat
9g sat fat | 53g protein | 4g carbs
3g sugar | 0.8g salt

2 x 2kg ducks
3 teaspoons five spice powder
2 teaspoons plain flour
2 tablespoons Shaoxing Chinese cooking wine or white wine
3–4 tablespoons Plum Sauce (see page 180)
200ml hot light chicken stock
salt and freshly ground black pepper
greens and roast potatoes, or steamed rice and pak choi, to serve

Prick the ducks all over with a fork. Sprinkle the ducks with the five spice powder and plenty of seasoning, inside and out, rubbing it in well. Place into a dish and chill for up to 2 hours (keeping in the fridge until 20 minutes before you are ready to cook).

Preheat the oven to 200°C/gas mark 6.

Transfer the ducks onto a wire rack placed in a deep roasting tin and roast the ducks for 1 ¾ hours. Check halfway through cooking and carefully pour or spoon some of the fat out of the tray.

Remove the ducks from the oven and increase the temperature to 220°C/gas mark 7. Transfer the ducks to a clean roasting tin and return them to the oven to crisp for a further 5 or so minutes.

Put the original roasting tin on the hob, spoon off any fat and discard, leaving about 1 tablespoon of fat and all the cooking juices. Then pour nearly all the remaining liquid into a jug. Add the flour to the tin and, using a wooden spoon, stir the tin over a medium heat to loosen any bits stuck on the bottom and to combine the flour. Remove the ducks from the oven and set aside to rest for 10 minutes. Add the Shaoxing wine or white wine to the tin and bubble over the heat, stirring, before gradually adding the reserved juices, plum sauce and chicken stock. Simmer gently for 5–10 minutes, stirring occasionally, then season with black pepper and taste (add more plum sauce for a fruitier gravy).

Carve the ducks and transfer the gravy to a serving jug.

For a Western slant, serve with some greens and roast potatoes, or for a healthier and more Asian version, accompany with steamed rice and pak choi, with the gravy to hand around.

KOREAN-STYLE SWEET & STICKY CHICKEN

There's nothing more delicious than tucking into sticky chicken straight from the oven. Andrew, my husband, is a fan of wings whereas the rest of us prefer legs, so I've given quantities for both. Either eat picnic-style or serve with some Healthy Fried Rice (see page 77). Great too for packed lunches! Lining the tray with baking parchment makes washing up the tin a doddle. You can also cook these on an oiled barbecue if you like.

Makes 6 drumsticks or 12 wings

PER DRUMSTICK: 163 cals | 5.5g fat
1.5g sat fat | 22g protein | 6g carbs
6g sugar | 1.2g salt

PER WING: 82 cals | 3.5g fat
0.9g sat fat | 9g protein | 3g carbs
3g sugar | 0.6g salt

6 chicken drumsticks or 12 wings
½ teaspoon sesame seeds

For the glaze
2 garlic cloves, crushed
1 tablespoon grated fresh ginger
2 tablespoons tamari or reduced-salt soy sauce
2 tablespoons clear honey, preferably raw
1 tablespoon rice vinegar
1 tablespoon sake, Shaoxing Chinese cooking wine or dry sherry (optional)
1 tablespoon low-salt and low-sugar tomato ketchup
freshly ground black pepper

Place the chicken in a shallow non-metallic dish. Mix all the ingredients for the glaze together in a small jug and pour half over the chicken along with a grinding of pepper, toss to coat. Cover and marinate in the fridge for 20 minutes to 24 hours.

Preheat the oven to 200°C/gas mark 6. Line a baking tray with baking parchment.

Put the chicken onto the tray. Bake the wings for 30–40 minutes and the drumsticks for 40–50 minutes, or until the chicken is cooked and brown. Brush with the extra sauce and turn the pieces about every 10 minutes, until all the sauce is used. Sprinkle with the sesame seeds for the final roasting.

BABY BACK RIBS WITH STICKY CITRUS GLAZE

Poaching the ribs not only melts away some of the fat but also tenderises them pre-grilling or barbecuing. You can make the glaze up to 2 days ahead and keep it in the fridge. Then poach the ribs, cool them down and let them sit in the glaze until you are ready to finish them.

Serves 4–6

PER SERVING (for 6): 254 cals | 14g fat
6.5g sat fat | 20g protein | 9g carbs
9g sugar | 0.9g salt

For the ribs
2 racks of baby back pork ribs, each cut in half
3 star anise
1 ½ tablespoons reduced-salt soy sauce
4 thick slices fresh ginger, peeled
½ red onion, cut into wedges

For the glaze
1 tablespoons light olive oil
1 small red onion, roughly chopped
2 teaspoons grated fresh ginger
3 large garlic cloves, crushed
1 large red chilli, deseeded (optional) and chopped
4 tablespoons good-quality hoisin sauce
2 tablespoons Shaoxing Chinese cooking wine, dry sherry, mirin or white wine
juice and zest of 2 large unwaxed oranges
salads, to serve (eg. Watercress, Asian Pear & Mint Salad on page 60 or Healthy Fried Rice on page 77)

Put the ribs into a large saucepan or sauté pan so that they fit in flat or slightly overlapping. Add the star anise, soy sauce, ginger and onion wedges, then cover with cold water. Bring to the boil, then simmer, covered, for 25–30 minutes, before draining the liquid off and leaving the ribs to cool.

For the glaze, heat the oil in a small pan and add the onion. Fry gently for 4–5 minutes to soften, then add the ginger, garlic and chilli (if using) and cook for a further 3–4 minutes. Add the remaining ingredients and simmer over a medium heat for 5 or so minutes, before turning off the heat and leaving to cool. Blitz with a stick blender or in a mini processor, then keep in a lidded container in the fridge until ready to use.

Once both the ribs and glaze are cool, place the ribs in a single layer in a shallow, non-metallic container, pour the glaze over, cover and chill in the fridge for up to 6 hours to marinate.

Remove the ribs from the fridge 30 minutes ahead of cooking. Preheat the barbecue or grill and cook the ribs over a medium heat for about 10 minutes, turning and brushing them with the glaze as they cook.

Serve with your chosen salad or Healthy Fried Rice.

ASIAN-STYLE PORK FILLET

Roast pork is sold everywhere in Singapore, in the markets and at the supermarket. It's a great ready-to-eat alternative to roast chicken to stuff into Vietnamese Summer Rolls (see page 35) or to add to stir-fried rice and noodles. Unfortunately for those who are keen to keep trim, it's usually pork belly – a tasty but fatty cut of pork. Here's a quick-to-prepare alternative, which will do the job for all of the above mentioned recipes, as well as being a great centrepiece.

Serve the fillet, sliced, with Watercress, Asian Pear & Mint Salad (see page 60) and perhaps a big bowl of soba noodles simply dressed with a little sesame oil and some toasted sesame seeds. If you want a sauce, simply make double the quantities of the marinade and heat until boiling for 3–4 minutes. Add a splash of water, taste for seasoning and serve spooned over the top.

Serves 4

PER SERVING: 260 cals | 10g fat | 3g sat fat
38g protein | 1.5g carbs | 1.5g sugar | 0g salt

juice and zest of ½ unwaxed orange
1 tablespoon sesame oil
3 garlic cloves, crushed
3 tablespoons Shaoxing Chinese cooking wine or dry sherry
1 ½ tablespoons hoisin sauce
1 tablespoon grated fresh ginger
½ teaspoon five spice powder
1 x 700g pork fillet, trimmed

Place all the ingredients, except the pork, in a non-metallic shallow dish and stir well to combine. Add the pork fillet and spoon over the marinade to coat. Cover and marinate in the fridge for 2 to 24 hours. (If you want extra sauce for serving, then make double the marinade, use a little for basting and then boil the rest in a pan for 3–4 minutes or until piping hot.)

Preheat the oven to 220°C/gas mark 7. Place a wire rack over a roasting tin and half-fill the tin with boiling water.

Remove the pork from the dish, scraping off and reserving the marinade. Place the pork on the wire rack and roast for 20 minutes.

Turn the fillet over and brush with the remaining marinade. Reduce the oven temperature to 170°C/gas mark 3 and cook for a further 5–15 minutes, depending on the thickness of the fillet (it should be just pink in the centre when sliced).

Remove from the oven, cover loosely with foil and set aside for 10 minutes to rest before slicing.

BRAISED PORK & PLUMS

What is so magical about Singapore is that though it is part of South-East Asia, because of its history there are many influences to the cooking here, including of course, a strong Chinese focus. Roast ducks hang from hooks at the market and dim sum can be eaten in a wide variety of establishments from 'queue at the door' stalwarts such as Din Tai Fung to the more luxurious hotels, such as the Goodwood Park Hotel.

Slow-cooked pork with the classic Chinese flavours of star anise, cinnamon, ginger and Shaoxing wine is a favourite of ours and I enjoy the freshness that the fruity plums add to the mix. However, in traditional recipes lots of sugar is often included to caramelise the meat and make a sweet sauce – although this is delicious, it's not a very healthy option. The sugar content appears high on the nutritional list, but most of it comes from the natural sugar in the plums and I've reduced the amount of sugar in the sauce and offered honey as an alternative – or if you prefer it can be missed out altogether. You'll notice one rather English addition – Worcestershire sauce – but it's worth it if you have it to hand. I like to serve the pork with nutritious red rice and some simply cooked Chinese greens. And if you've got any leftover, it freezes really well.

Serves 4-5

Per serving (for 5): 370 cals | 9g fat 3g sat fat | 47g protein | 21g carbs 17.5g sugar | 1.3g salt

1kg lean pork shoulder, cut into 5–6cm cubes

For the marinade
5cm piece of fresh ginger, peeled and thinly sliced into rounds
4 garlic cloves, finely chopped
1 large green chilli, deseeded and sliced
1 tablespoon light soy sauce
1 tablespoon reduced-salt dark soy sauce
1 tablespoon Worcestershire sauce (optional)
1 1/2 teaspoons cornflour
5 tablespoons Shaoxing Chinese cooking wine or dry sherry

For the sauce
spray oil
2 small red onions, cut into wedges
1–2 tablespoons palm sugar or honey, preferably raw
1 cinnamon stick
3 star anise
8 dark plums, stoned and quartered
300ml hot low-salt chicken stock
2 leeks, cut on the diagonal into 4cm thick pieces
steamed red or jasmine rice and Chinese greens, to serve

Put the pork into a non-metallic, shallow container with the ginger, garlic, chilli, soy sauces, Worcestershire sauce (if using), cornflour and half the wine. Stir together, cover and leave to marinate in the fridge for 30 minutes to 24 hours. Preheat the oven to 170°C/gas mark 3.

Spray some oil into a large, ovenproof casserole, over a low–medium heat and add the onions. Cook, stirring every so often, for 8–10 minutes, then add the palm sugar or honey and stir for 1–2 minutes or until the sugar dissolves.

Drain the pork, reserving any leftover marinade. Increase the heat in the casserole, add the pork and cook for 2–3 minutes, stirring occasionally, to seal the meat. Add the remaining wine and reserved marinade and bring up to a simmer. Add the cinnamon stick and star anise, two-thirds of the plums and the stock. Bring to the boil, then cover and transfer to the oven for 2 hours.

After 2 hours, add the remaining plums and leeks and return to the oven for a further 10–15 minutes or until the leeks are cooked and the meat is tender. Serve with steamed red or jasmine rice and Chinese greens.

BRAISED BEEF WITH MUSHROOMS

This is a comforting recipe. Although it includes Asian flavours, and suits a serving of brown rice and Asian greens, it would equally be suited to some mashed potatoes and peas on the side. It's also even better if cooked the day before and then reheated as this allows the flavours to develop. Remove from the fridge about an hour before you want to serve it, allow to stand at room temperature for 15 minutes, and preheat the oven to 170°C/gas mark 3. Cover the casserole and reheat in the oven for 45 minutes or so or until piping hot.

I recently read an amazing book called *Anticancer: A New Way of Life* by David Servan-Schreiber, which talked about shiitake mushrooms and their superfood properties, so this recipe is a winner on the healthy eating stakes too.

Having non-stick casseroles and pans certainly helps when trying to keep things healthy as there's less tendency for things to stick, which normally means extra oil required!

Serves 6

Per serving: 400 cals | 16.5g fat
8.5g sat fat | 51g protein | 7g carbs
6g sugar | 1.3g salt

1 ½kg braising beef (preferably shin), trimmed and cut into 5cm cubes
2 tablespoons reduced-salt soy sauce
100ml Shaoxing Chinese cooking wine or dry sherry
2–3 tablespoons coconut or light olive oil
4 garlic cloves, thinly sliced
10cm piece of fresh ginger, peeled and grated
12 whole shallots
2 long red chillies, deseeded and thinly sliced
1 teaspoon five spice powder
½ teaspoon ground cinnamon
2 tablespoons plain flour
3 star anise
1 tablespoon clear honey, preferably raw
1 tablespoon tomato purée
500ml hot beef stock
3 bay leaves
100g shiitake mushrooms
100g button chestnut mushrooms
salt and freshly ground black pepper
brown rice and stir-fried greens, to serve

Place the beef in a non-metallic container, add the soy sauce , wine or sherry and some black pepper. Cover with clingfilm and refrigerate for at least 1 hour or preferably overnight, to marinate. When ready to cook, preheat the oven to 150°C/gas mark 2.

Drain the beef in a colander over a bowl and reserve the marinade. Dry the beef with kitchen paper and season with salt. Add 1 tablespoon of the oil to a large casserole over a medium heat, then brown the meat in batches until starting to caramelise, adding a little extra oil if needed. Transfer to a bowl using a slotted spoon.

Heat ½ tablespoon of the oil in the casserole. Fry the garlic, ginger, shallots and chillies for 4–5 minutes or until they start to colour. Then add the five spice powder and cinnamon and cook for 1 minute. Return the beef to the casserole and stir in the flour and some salt and pepper. Mix the star anise, honey, tomato purée and stock with the reserved marinade in the bowl until well combined. Slowly add this mixture to the beef and vegetables, add the bay leaves and then bring to the boil and cover tightly. Transfer the casserole to the oven for 2 ½ hours, stir after 1 ¼ hours and add the mushrooms after 2 hours. Season to taste and serve with brown rice and stir-fried greens.

STEAKS 'BULGOGI' STYLE

This is one of Korea's most popular dishes – finely sliced beef marinated in a garlic, soy sauce, sugar and sesame combination and then barbecued. This recipe uses a similar marinade to traditional recipes, but without the vast amount of sugar and salt usually included in classic versions. I've also opted for whole steaks, which are barbecued and then sliced. If you want the steaks to have a fiery kick, then include a sprinkle of chilli flakes in the marinade.

I like to serve this with salad and it works especially well with Sugar Snap, Sesame & Orange Salad (see page 60) or Rainbow Slaw with Peanut Dressing (see page 58).

Serves 4

PER SERVING: 292 cals | 10.5g fat | 4g sat fat 47g protein | 2g carbs | 2g sugar | 1.4g salt

2 large garlic cloves, crushed
1 ½ tablespoons light soy sauce, reduced-salt soy sauce or tamari
2 teaspoons clear honey, preferably raw
2 teaspoons sesame oil
⅓ teaspoon cayenne pepper
⅓ teaspoon dried chilli flakes (optional)
4 lean sirloin or ribeye steaks
salt and freshly ground black pepper
Sugar Snap, Sesame & Orange Salad (see page 60) or Rainbow Slaw with Peanut Dressing (see page 58), to serve

In a small jug, mix together the garlic, soy sauce, honey, sesame oil, cayenne pepper, chilli flakes (if using) and a good grinding of black pepper. Place the steaks in a non-metallic shallow container. Rub the marinade all over the steaks, cover and marinate in the fridge for 30 minutes to 3 hours.

Heat the barbecue, season the steaks with salt, then cook for 3-4 minutes on each side or until cooked to your liking. Alternatively, heat a griddle pan to smoking hot, brush the beef with a little oil and griddle for 3-5 minutes on each side or until cooked to your liking. Leave to rest for 10 minutes on a chopping board, before slicing and serving with your choice of salad.

ASIAN SPICED LAMB WITH PUMPKIN & CRUSHED PEAS WITH FRESH MINT

Though lamb is not eaten much in Asia, this recipe, developed by my health wiz assistant Charlotte, is a delicious example of how East meets West can work and can be a healthy option too. Don't be put off by the long list of ingredients, as many are store cupboard ingredients. Plus, so much can be prepared ahead that it's a great option for entertaining too. The minted peas have just a hint of heat from the wasabi, but simply leave it out if you prefer a milder flavour.

Serves 6

PER SERVING: 386 cals | 23g fat | 13g sat fat 35g protein | 9g carbs | 4.5g sugar 0.4g salt

For the lamb and sauce
1 ½ teaspoons ground turmeric
1 ½ teaspoons ground cumin
1 ½ teaspoons ground coriander
½ teaspoons hot chilli powder
juice of 1 lime
1 teaspoon light olive oil
½ teaspoon flaked sea salt
12 trimmed lamb cutlets
2 garlic cloves, crushed
200ml light coconut milk
200ml hot chicken stock
2 tablespoons chopped coriander leaves

For the roast pumpkin
1 kg pumpkin or butternut squash (unprepared weight), peeled and cut into 2cm cubes
1 tablespoon coconut or light olive oil

For the peas
450g frozen baby peas, defrosted
30g mint leaves
1 tablespoon light olive oil
1 tablespoon wasabi paste (optional)
2 spring onions, trimmed and finely chopped
salt and freshly ground black pepper

Preheat the oven to 200°C/gas mark 6.

For the lamb, mix together the ground spices, chilli powder, half the lime juice, oil and salt. Pat the lamb dry, place it in a shallow non-metallic container and rub about half of the spice paste all over the cutlets, reserving any remaining paste. Cover and chill for up to 2 hours.

For the roast pumpkin, put the pumpkin cubes into a shallow roasting tray in a single layer (you can cut these up to 2 hours ahead and keep in a food bag in the fridge). Toss the pumpkin with the oil along with a good sprinkle of salt and pepper. Roast for 10–15 minutes or until just soft but still holding its shape.

Recipe continues overleaf...

Place the defrosted peas, mint, oil, wasabi (if using), spring onions and a good pinch of salt and pepper in a food processor and blitz until almost smooth – it is nice to leave a little bit of pea texture. You can chill this up to 2 hours ahead, but bring back to room temperature before serving.

Heat a large heavy-based, non-stick frying pan. When hot, place each cutlet, fat-side down in the pan, to render the fat for 1–2 minutes (pour off any residual fat). Then lay the cutlets flat in the pan and cook for 3 minutes on each side for medium-rare or until cooked to your liking. Remove the lamb from pan and leave to rest.

Mix the garlic with the remaining spice mix. Add to the pan and fry for 30 seconds before adding the coconut milk and stock. Let the sauce bubble for a couple of minutes so it reduces and thickens. Add salt and pepper to taste. Turn off the heat and stir in the remaining lime juice.

Spoon the roasted pumpkin onto plates and place two cutlets on top. Drizzle some of the coconut sauce over the lamb, add a good dollop of minted peas on the side and sprinkle with fresh coriander. Serve any remaining sauce separately.

BURGERS THREE WAYS

THAI LAMB BURGERS WITH TOMATO AND MINT SALAD

Lean lamb mince is the perfect meat for the barbecue. Choose good-quality or mince your own to make sure it is not too fatty. Thai flavours and a bit of heat from the curry paste are also a great combination with the refreshing tomato and mint salad to heap on top. Adding grated courgette to both lamb and beef burgers is my great healthy trick as it adds extra nutrition, means you use less meat and keeps the burgers really moist. You can use a barbecue or griddle pan to cook these.

Makes 6 burgers

Per burger: 369 cals | 20g fat | 7.5g sat fat 20.5g protein | 26g carbs | 4g sugar 0.8g salt

For the burgers
500g lean lamb mince
2 spring onions, finely chopped
2 tablespoons Thai Red Curry Paste (see page 174)
½ large courgette, grated
2 tablespoons chopped mint leaves
¾ teaspoon sea salt flakes
2 teaspoons coconut or light olive oil

For the salad
3 tomatoes, quartered, deseeded and cut into slivers
3 small shallots, finely chopped
1 ½ tablespoons chopped mint leaves
1 ½ tablespoons light olive oil
1 ½ tablespoons lime juice
6 ciabatta rolls, to serve

To make the burgers, combine the mince with the spring onions, Thai red curry paste, courgette, mint and salt. Form into 6 patties, transfer to a tray, then cover and chill for at least 3 hours.

Preheat the barbecue or a griddle pan to very hot. Brush the burgers and barbecue grill or griddle with the oil and place the burgers on. Once sealed on both sides, lower the heat or carefully move them over to a medium heat area and cook for a further 10-12 minutes, turning over carefully, until cooked to your liking.

For the salad, combine the tomatoes, shallots, mint, oil and lime juice in a medium bowl with some seasoning and serve with the burgers and rolls.

JAPANESE-STYLE CHICKEN BURGERS

Super easy to prepare ahead of a gathering, these flavour-packed chicken burgers can be served simply in buns (I like ciabatta) with some Japanese mayonnaise, Sweet & Sour Cucumber Salad (see page 54) and lettuce or without buns with the Soba Noodle & Edamame Salad (see page 72). If you don't have the barbecue out, simply pan-fry over a low–medium heat (so the honey doesn't catch) in a lightly oiled frying pan or griddle.

Makes 4 burgers

PER BURGER: 436 cals | 7.5g fat | 1g sat fat 44.5g protein | 48g carbs | 13g sugar 2.5g salt

4 chicken breasts
1 quantity Teriyaki marinade (see page 105)
2 teaspoons light olive oil

To serve
½ quantity Sweet & Sour Cucumber Salad (see page 54)
4 burger buns or Soba Noodle & Edamame Salad (see page 72)
small handful of cos, gem or iceburg lettuce, shredded
1 heaped tablespoon mayonnaise

Sandwich the chicken breasts in clingfilm and bash them on a board using a rolling pin to even them out and flatten slightly. Place in a shallow non-metallic container and pour over the teriyaki marinade to coat. Cover and chill for up to 2 hours.

Preheat the barbecue or a frying pan or griddle. Drain the chicken from the marinade and brush the breasts with the oil. Cook the chicken on a very hot part of the barbecue, in the frying pan or on the griddle for 3–4 minutes on each side until just cooked through. Serve with the Sweet & Sour Cucumber Salad or in buns with shredded salad and mayonnaise.

VIETNAMESE-STYLE PORK PATTIES

These are a great party food as they can be made small enough to pick up in your fingers or larger to serve as a main course. Serve them with the Watercress, Asian Pear & Mint Salad (see page 60) and a bowl of Nuoc Cham Dipping Sauce (page 180).

Makes 14 small patties or 6 medium burgers

PER MEDIUM BURGER: 140 cals | 8g fat 3g sat fat | 16g protein | 0.5g carbs 0.5g sugar | 0.9g salt

500g lean pork mince
1 small garlic clove, chopped
2 spring onions, finely chopped
1 lemongrass stalk, tough outer leaves removed and remaining inner stalk very finely chopped
a small bunch of coriander, leaves and stems chopped
1 tablespoon chopped mint
1 ½ tablespoon fish sauce
zest of 1 unwaxed lime
½ long red chilli, with seeds, finely chopped
spray oil or light olive oil, for brushing
salt and freshly ground black pepper
Asian Pear and Salad (page 60), Nuoc Cham Dipping Sauce (page 180) and bread, to serve

Mix together the pork mince, garlic, spring onions, lemongrass, coriander, mint, fish sauce, lime zest and chilli along with some salt and black pepper. With wet hands, form the mixture into 14 bite-sized or 6 larger patties. Place on a tray, cover and chill in the fridge for a minimum of 3 hours or in the freezer for 20 minutes.

Spray or brush the patties with oil. Preheat the barbecue or the grill to medium–high. Cook the patties for 8–12 minutes, depending on size, turning once or twice, or until cooked through. Serve with the salad, dipping sauce and bread.

Drinks & Sweet Treats

What to pour for drinks and what to serve for pudding are the two tricky questions when it comes to eating and matching Asian food, so I've worked hard on this chapter to offer some clever ideas that are healthy too. The answer is, on the whole, to keep it fresh and simple.

Although alcohol is not something naturally connected to healthy eating, I'm also not a total purist, and a fresh and zingy Lime Mint Vodka Cooler made with fresh limes and soda to kick off a summer evening is certainly a healthier option than beers or gin and tonics.

One of the upsides of living in Asia is the variety of bright and delicious fruits available all year round. For me, nothing can beat a platter of Summery Fruit Salad with Lime, Lemongrass & Mint Dressing as the perfect palette cleanser after a spicy meal. Though perhaps a little cheaper here, all the fruits used are available all over the world too, and also don't feel you can't swap for a seasonal equivalent – strawberries, raspberries or nectarines to name just a few.

Equally there is always a time for chocolate and richer puds, and it would not be right if I didn't embrace native Asian's passion for sweet treats – with shops full of stunning cakes and ice cream on every corner. There are clever things you can do to keep the fat and sugar down though, so don't feel too guilty if you do fancy trying the Vietnamese-style Chocolate & Coffee Pots, Summer Coconut Rice with Pineapple or Spiced Banana & Coconut Loaf!

VIETNAMESE-STYLE CHOCOLATE & COFFEE POTS

The Vietnamese serve heart-racingly strong coffee that usually arrives with a little metal filter on top and a glass of condensed milk on the side, which sinks to the bottom of the cup and gives a delicious sweet creamy rush. These fun little puds are Vietnamese-inspired chocolate pots.

Makes 8 x 50ml glasses

Per serving (for 8): 55 cals | 2.5g fat
1.5g sat fat | 2g protein | 6g carbs
6g sugar | 0.1g salt

100g dark chocolate, minimum 60% cocoa solids, broken into pieces, plus extra for decoration
2 teaspoons cocoa powder
2 tablespoons condensed milk
5 tablespoons hot, very strong espresso coffee
3 free-range egg whites
½ teaspoon lemon juice

Put the chocolate, cocoa powder and condensed milk into a medium heatproof bowl and melt over a pan of just simmering water. Remove from the heat (it will be quite thick at this stage). While it is still hot, stir in the just-made hot coffee. Set aside to cool for 15 minutes.

Whisk the egg whites in a clean medium bowl with the lemon juice until they form stiff peaks. Stir 1 large spoonful into the cooled chocolate mixture to loosen it, then fold the remaining whites into the chocolate mixture. Divide between 8 espresso cups or pretty glasses. Chill until ready to serve.

Grate some dark chocolate over the top before serving.

PASSION FRUIT & ORANGE WATER ICE

In Asia, the passion fruit are enormous and often not wrinkled like the ones in the UK. I saw a lady at the market who was buying so many that I nosily asked her what she was using them for. She told me that she makes a quick healthy sorbet using only whizzed-up passion fruit pulp. She spoons it into ice-cube trays and freezes it for her children. This is a variation of her recipe, which avoids the high quantities of sugar that sorbets and granitas can traditionally contain. However, because of this it is slightly more icy but seriously refreshing. If you like it less tart, add a little more water and honey.

Makes approximately 1 litre

(V) (GF) (DF) (LF)

Per 100ml: 55 cals | 0g fat | 0g sat fat
1g protein | 12g carbs | 12g sugar | 0g salt

8 large ripe passion fruit, or 10–12 small (to yield 300ml pulp)
600ml orange juice (about 6 large oranges)
finely grated zest of 1 unwaxed orange
finely grated zest and juice of 1 unwaxed lime
2–3 tablespoons clear honey, preferably raw

Push the passion fruit pulp through a sieve into a bowl and then, for a crunchy water ice, return as many of the pips as you like to the liquid; for a smooth texture, leave the pips out. Add the orange juice and zest and lime juice and zest, 2 tablespoons of the honey and 350ml of cold water to the bowl and stir together. Taste for sweetness, adding more honey as required.

Pour into an ice-cream maker and churn until three-quarters frozen, then transfer to a freezerproof lidded container and freeze until solid.

If you don't have an ice-cream maker, pour the mixture into a deep, narrow freezerproof lidded container and freeze. Break up the ice crystals 2–3 times during freezing, by either whizzing in a food processor, or using a hand-held electric blender or a fork, every couple of hours. The more often you break up the crystals the less grainy it will be.

Remove the water ice from the freezer a few minutes before serving.

FRESH AND SPEEDY LIME & MANGO YOGURT ICE

So, the speedy part is the preparation, which literally takes 5 minutes. The rest is taken care of by a freezer or ideally an ice-cream maker. I suggest serving smallish portions as a perfect after-dinner ice cream with a heap of raspberries or a fresh berry purée on the side. It is also delicious served as a semifreddo, in which case, freeze the ice cream until it is three-quarters frozen, then ripple through the mango just before serving it into bowls. Or you can pour the rippled mixture into a clingfilm-lined loaf tin (crunched up meringue would be a delicious addition), then freeze and serve turned onto a platter and sliced.

Serves 10–12

(V) (GF) (LF)

Per serving (for 12): 150 cals | 2.5g fat
1.5g sat fat | 6g protein | 25g carbs
25g sugar | 0.3g salt

400g full-fat Greek yogurt
300g low-fat plain yogurt
zest of 4 unwaxed limes
405g can condensed milk or light condensed milk
150ml lime juice (4–6 juicy limes)
1 medium ripe mango, peeled and cut into chunks

Spoon the Greek yogurt into a bowl, add the plain yogurt and sprinkle over the lime zest. Fold together. Drizzle over the condensed milk, folding it in as you pour. Then gradually fold in the lime juice until just mixed.

Pour into an ice-cream maker and churn until three-quarters frozen, then transfer to a freezerproof lidded container. If you don't have an ice-cream maker, pour the mixture into a deep, narrow freezerproof lidded container and freeze. Break up the ice crystals 2–3 times during freezing, by either whizzing in a food processor or using a hand-held electric blender until the yogurt is three-quarters frozen.

Purée the mango and, using a large metal spoon, fold in the purée just enough so that it ripples through the ice cream, then freeze for the final time.

Remove from the freezer 10–20 minutes before serving.

DRINKS & SWEET TREATS

SUMMERY FRUIT SALAD WITH LIME, LEMONGRASS & MINT DRESSING

There are endless possibilities for this beautiful salad, as the fruits you choose will depend on where you live and what's in season. However, the simple aromatic dressing is a winner for most fresh fruits, so you can't really go wrong. Thank-you Caz for the inspiration.

Serves 6

PER SERVING: 120cals | 0g fat | 0g sat fat 1.5g protein | 27g carbs | 27g sugar | 0g salt

For the dressing

3 slices of fresh ginger
1 ½ tablespoons clear honey
zest of 2 unwaxed limes
1 lemongrass stalk, bashed with a rolling pin, then cut into chunks
juice of 1 lime

For the fruit salad

1 ripe mango or papaya, peeled, stoned and cut into chunks
½ ripe pineapple, peeled, cored and cut into chunks
2 kiwi fruit, peeled and cut into half moons
⅛ large watermelon (about 800g unprepared weight), peeled and cut into chunks
6 longans or lychees, cut into small chunks
small bunch of mint

For the dressing, pour 150ml of cold water into a small pan with the ginger, honey, lime zest and lemongrass. Bring up to a simmer and bubble gently for about 3-5 minutes or until the liquid has reduced to about 100ml. Strain through a sieve into a jug, discard the ginger and lemongrass, and stir in the lime juice, to taste. The dressing should be sweet but sharp. Set aside to cool.

Place the prepared fruit in a serving bowl. Pour the dressing over the fruit and stir together. Cover and chill in the fridge until ready to serve. Just before serving, chop the mint leaves, add to the fruit and stir well.

BANANAS COOKED IN COCONUT MILK

My children are still big fans of traditional English nursery food like banana custard and rice pudding. This is my Asian equivalent – warm bananas bathed in honey-sweetened coconut and cinnamon sauce. My children are addicts, as our grown-up guests often are and, unlike the classic banana custard, this is made with natural ingredients. My preference is to use full-fat coconut milk for this, as it does add a richness to the pudding, but if you are watching the calories, then use light. Don't forget the important pinch of salt to balance the flavours.

Serves 2–3

PER SERVING (FOR 3 USING LIGHT COCONUT MILK): 182 cals | 5g fat | 4g sat fat 2g protein | 33g carbs | 30g sugar | 0g salt

200ml coconut milk or light coconut milk
1 cinnamon stick
2 tablespoons clear honey
2 firm, large bananas, sliced diagonally into 2cm pieces
flaked sea salt

Gently heat the coconut milk in a small pan with 4 tablespoons of cold water, the cinnamon and honey until simmering, then cook for 3 minutes. Add the bananas and a pinch of salt and cook the bananas in the milk for a further 3 minutes, ensuring that they don't go soft. Serve immediately.

SUMMER COCONUT RICE WITH PINEAPPLE

The combination of brown rice and short grain pudding rice in this simple chilled dessert is perfect as the wholegrain brown rice is high in fibre and nutrients and adds a nutty flavour and the short-grain rice gives the requisite creaminess. Serve in pretty cups or tea glasses, topped with the fruit or send to school in lidded pots for healthy and tasty children's packed lunches. Alternatively, serve straight from the pan with a drizzle of purée on the top. Any chopped fruit that you choose can go on the top – pineapple, mango, poached plums or peaches – whatever you fancy or have in the fruit bowl.

Serves 8 (V) (VE)   (GF) (DF) (LF)

PER SERVING: 139 cals | 4g fat | 3g sat fat
3g protein | 23g carbs | 11g sugar

60g short-grain brown rice
1 cinnamon stick
60g short- or medium-grain white rice such as pudding rice or risotto rice
400ml can light coconut milk
400ml skimmed milk
50g palm sugar, chopped or grated
2 teaspoons vanilla extract
4 ripe, fresh pineapple slices, cored and cut into 1cm cubes

Boil the kettle. Rinse the brown rice and soak it in cold water for 5 minutes, then drain. Place the brown rice in a pan with the cinnamon and 450ml of freshly boiled water. Simmer for about 25 minutes.

Add the white rice to the pan, pour in the coconut milk and skimmed milk, and add the sugar and vanilla extract. Bring up to a simmer and cook gently, stirring occasionally, for about 40–50 minutes or until the rice is soft. It should be quite liquidy, as the rice will continue to soak up the liquid as it chills. Transfer to 8 little pots or cups, so that the pudding reaches three-quarters of the way up. Top with the pineapple, then chill for at least 2 hours.

POACHED JASMINE PEARS

Jasmine tea is commonly green tea that has jasmine flowers added. It can be a little confusing however because you can also buy jasmine tea which has been mixed with white and black tea, plus of course pure green tea and green tea with other flavourings added – so do check the label! Green tea is the one with super powers though, and we should all be ideally drinking it from dawn until dusk to reap its anti-cancer properties. Start by putting it in the poaching liquid for these delicious pears. We like them not overly sweet, but feel free to add more sugar if you like a slightly thicker syrup. Soft light brown sugar is the best alternative to palm sugar in this recipe. Serve with a little vanilla ice cream on the side, if you like.

Serves 4 (V) (VE) (GF) (DF) (LF)

PER SERVING: 81 cals | 0g fat | 0g sat fat
0.5g protein | 19g carbs | 14g sugar | 0g salt

4 firm European pears, such as Bosc
2 good-quality jasmine teabags or 6–7 jasmine and green tea pearls
1½ heaped tablespoons palm sugar, finely chopped or grated
4 thin slices fresh ginger, peeled
vanilla ice cream, to serve

Peel and carefully halve the pears, then, using the sharp point of a knife, remove the central core by making a neat round hole.

Meanwhile, bring 600ml of cold water up to the boil in a pan just large enough to fit the pears in a snug single layer. Add the teabags or pearls, sugar and ginger to the boiling water. Leave the tea to steep for 5 minutes, then remove the teabags but leave the pearls in, add the pears and simmer gently, uncovered, for 25–30 minutes or until the pears are just tender, turning in the poaching liquid once.

Remove the pears from the liquid and, if needed, reduce the remaining liquid a little by boiling for a little longer – it should resemble a light syrup. Serve the pears with a little of the syrup poured over and a scoop of vanilla ice cream.

SPICED BANANA & COCONUT LOAF

Bananas are super cheap to buy in Asia and the mini ones taste delicious. If they go black, which they tend to do in the blink of an eye, I turn them into healthy banana cake as the loaves freeze well and are a great tea-time quick fix for play dates and hungry children. My two love a slice warm from the oven with some fresh mango.

I often make this in a double batch, using my hand-held blender to mush up a heap of banana in one go. The loaves freeze beautifully both in slices and as whole cakes. I buy a fine, wholemeal flour that goes through my sieve but if you find you can't sieve it, just sprinkle it from a height to get as much air into the mixture as possible. I sometimes add a handful of sultanas to the mixture, in which case add an extra tablespoon of coconut milk.

Makes 10 thick slices

PER SLICE: 242cals | 12g fat | 2g sat fat
5g protein | 30g carbs | 14g sugar
0.3g salt

3 regular or 10 mini over-ripe bananas (about 300g flesh)
5–6 tablespoons light coconut milk
125ml coconut or light olive oil
100ml clear honey, preferably raw
2 medium free-range eggs
1 ½ teaspoons vanilla extract
75g plain flour, sifted
150g finely ground plain wholemeal flour, sifted
10g chia seeds
2 teaspoons baking powder
½ teaspoon five spice powder
¾ teaspoon ground cinnamon
1 tablespoon shredded coconut (optional)

Preheat the oven to 170°C/gas mark 3. Grease and line a 900g loaf tin.

Mash the bananas thoroughly with a fork or hand-held electric blender.

Put the coconut milk (5 tablespoons if not adding shredded coconut, otherwise add 6), oil, honey, eggs and vanilla into a large bowl and whisk together until combined. Stir in the mashed banana.

In a separate bowl, lightly mix together the flours, chia seeds, baking powder, five spice powder, cinnamon and coconut (if using), with a fork. Sprinkle the dry ingredients over the oil and egg mixture and fold in using a large metal spoon until just combined. Turn into the prepared tin and bake on the middle shelf for 50–55 minutes or until rich brown in colour and a skewer inserted into the middle of the cake comes out clean.

Leave in the tin for 5 minutes, then turn onto a wire rack. Leave for at least 15 minutes or until cool before slicing.

DRINKS & SWEET TREATS

LEMONGRASS & GINGER FIZZ

Due to the constant heat and humidity in Singapore we often resort to long drinks with lots of ice in order to keep cool and hydrated, and this is the Petch family's favourite recipe.

If you are a ginger lover, try to get hold of fresh young ginger as it adds the most wonderful clean heat. You can also use ginger beer as opposed to ale, if you prefer a bit more heat. Adding vodka also gives this a delicious grown-up twist.

Makes 1.85 litres / serves 5

PER SERVING: 38 cals | 0g fat | 0g sat fat
0g protein | 9g carbs | 9g sugar | 0g salt

5cm piece fresh ginger, peeled and cut into slivers
  using a peeler
2 lemongrass stalks, each cut into 3 and lightly bashed
2 tablespoons clear honey, preferably raw or maple syrup
2 unwaxed lemons
ice
1 litre sparkling or soda water
650ml ginger ale or ginger beer

Boil the kettle. Place the ginger, lemongrass and honey into a heatproof jug. Squeeze the juice from the lemons into the jug and then cut the halves into quarters and add them. Pour over 125ml of boiling water and pound everything together with the end of a rolling pin or pestle. Leave to infuse for as long as possible.

To serve, either remove the aromatics, or for a more rustic drink, simply transfer everything to a large jug. Add plenty of ice. Pour over the water and ginger ale or beer. Give a gentle stir with a wooden spoon and pour into glasses, using a small strainer or slotted spoon.

WATERMELON & COCONUT JUICE

This drink is super refreshing and appealing to children due to its beautiful colour and natural sweetness. Coconut water is the clear liquid inside young green coconuts (different to coconut milk, which is the liquid that comes from the ground-up white coconut flesh, once squeezed). Coconut water is a 'buzz' food right now as it contains large amounts of potassium and magnesium, is low in calories and high in electrolytes – to hydrate you naturally. Watermelon is also hydrating and has numerous vitamins. It's great in a juice as you need nothing more than a stick blender to blitz it.

Makes about 1.2 litres / serves 6

PER SERVING: 49 cals | 0g fat | 0.9g protein
9g carbs | 9g sugar | 0g salt

1 piece of watermelon weighing 1kg with skin on or about 700g once skin and black pips removed, chopped into 5cm chunks
600ml coconut water
2–3 tablespoons lime juice
ice, to serve

Put the watermelon into a jug or blender with the coconut water and lime juice. Blend or use a stick blender to blitz the watermelon until it is completely smooth. Pour into a jug, straining through a sieve if you prefer a completely smooth texture. Chill untill really cold. Add plenty of ice and serve.

VIETNAMESE ICED COFFEE

As explained in the intro for the chocolate pots, in Vietnam they make their coffee very strong and sweeten it with condensed milk. Serving it over ice cubes is a great way to enjoy it and will satisfy my desire to include iced coffee in this book due to the Asians' love of it, without having to make it too fattening!

Serves 4

Per serving: 24 cals | 0.5g fat | 0.1g sat fat
1g protein | 5g carbs | 5g sugar | 0g salt

600ml strong coffee
2–4 tablespoons light condensed milk
ice, to serve

Make the coffee and stir in the condensed milk to taste – I would put about ½ tablespoon per glass, but it is up to the individual. Chill for as long as you can, then pour over glasses full of ice.

LIME MINT
VODKA COOLER

I'm not a big fan of mixing random ingredients into drinks to make them fit a theme – so there won't be any funny business going on with this cocktail! However, the combination of fresh kaffir lime and mint leaves added to vodka is a match made in heaven and instantly transports you to somewhere tropical and tranquil – as long as you have your eyes shut when you drink it!

Serves 4–6

Per serving (for 6): 163 cals | 0g fat
0g sat fat | 0g protein | 8.5g carbs
8.5g sugar |0g salt

350ml vodka
5 fresh or 8 dried kaffir lime leaves
12 mint sprigs, plus extra to serve
75ml lime juice (2–3 juicy limes)
2 limes, cut into wedges, plus extra to serve
handful of ice, plus extra to serve
sugar syrup or stevia syrup, to taste (see Tip)
1–1.2 litres soda water

If you have enough time, add the lime leaves to the vodka a day or two in advance so that their flavour gently infuses into the alcohol. Put the vodka into a jug with the kaffir lime leaves, mint leaves, lime juice and lime wedges and bash with the end of a rolling pin to release the flavours and the juice.

Add a handful of ice, then add a dash of sugar syrup or stevia and some soda water and mix. Taste and add extra lime or soda and sweeten as required, then pour into long glasses half-filled with ice and throw in a couple of lime wedges and some extra mint.

Tip: Traditionally, sugar syrup is made by dissolving 2 parts sugar in 1 part water. Alternatively, for this recipe you can use bottled liquid stevia to taste, or 4 x 1g sachets of powdered stevia dissolved in the lime juice instead.

THE PERFECT CUP OF JASMINE (GREEN) TEA

It's not rocket science, I know, but it is worth mentioning that making a perfect cup of jasmine green tea or green tea does rely first and foremost on the quality of tea purchased. Look for the tea pearls that you can buy from supermarkets, delis or online these days. Not only are they made from better-quality, larger leaves, but they look beautiful as they unravel in the cup too. If not, just buy the best loose tea or teabags that you can.

And to make the perfect brew? Well, I've been taught that you should always put a dash of cold water in the pot or cup of freshly boiled water before adding the tea. That way the water is just off boiling and will not scorch the tea when it comes into contact with the water (this is what makes tea bitter). Then simply leave it to brew for 3–4 minutes, strain into a cup or remove the teabag straightaway and drink.

ICED LEMON TEA

Iced lemon tea is hugely popular over here in Asia, where all the restaurants and cafés seem to have lemon tea dispensers. I really enjoy it but unfortunately it's far from healthy as it contains a huge amount of sugar. It is, however, easy enough to make at home and you can also adjust all the elements to suit your taste. Try it the traditional way, made with good-quality orange pekoe tea or as I enjoy it, made from green tea with jasmine. You can sweeten the tea while hot with a sprinkling of stevia or honey to taste.

Serves 4

(V) (LG) (GF) (DF) (LS) (LF)

PER SERVING: 26 cals | 0g fat | 0g sat fat
0g protein | 6g carbs | 6g sugar | 0g salt

tea leaves, preferably green tea, or orange pekoe or jasmine
juice of 1 lemon
honey or stevia, to sweeten
lemon slices and ice, to serve

Boil the kettle and make the tea using 700ml of boiled water (see packet instructions for how much tea is needed). Remove the teabags or strain the leaves after 3–4 minutes. Add the lemon juice and sweeten to taste. Leave the tea to cool at room temperature to prevent it going cloudy. Add some lemon slices and plenty of ice and serve.

Tip: For a more fruity affair, add chopped strawberries, orange, grapes and kiwi and serve with a spoon.

Basics: Rice, Stock, Dressings, Pickles, Pastes & Sauces

This is the equivalent to the basics chapter in a Western cookbook – the section that holds up the rest of the book as without it you can't make half the dishes! But, wow, this is certainly a more exciting chapter than one which gives you recipes for a standard béchamel sauce, pastry or mayonnaise.

Chillies, lemongrass, lime leaves, herbs and spices keep this chapter alive with flavour, zing and vibrance! And as you will see, the recipes all contain good-for-you ingredients, which we are all told to eat as many of as possible – antioxidant, anticancer, antibacterial – and that's just the antis!

Just a word to reassure you – although the paste ingredients lists are long, please don't fear as the methods are short! And once you've made a batch it will keep in your fridge or freezer for ages. Please experiment with the dipping sauces, marinades and dressings; they are designed to be played around with and the recipes in this book are just the first of hopefully many varieties you will try.

COOKING WHITE LONG-GRAIN RICE (WHITE, JASMINE OR BASMATI)

200g uncooked rice will make approx. 2 servings

Wash the rice twice in cold water then drain. Use 1 volume of rice (i.e. 200ml) to 1¹/2 just-boiled water (i.e. 300ml). Put the drained rice into a pan and top with the water. Bring to the boil, cover with a lid and gently boil for 10 minutes. Turn off the heat, remove the lid and cover the pan with a folded tea towel. Leave to stand for 5 minutes before fluffing with a fork.

COOKING BROWN LONG-GRAIN RICE

200g uncooked rice will make approx. 2 servings

Wash the rice twice in cold water then drain. Use 1 volume of rice (i.e. 200ml) to 3¹/2 just-boiled water (i.e. 700ml). Put the drained rice into a pan and top with the water. Bring to the boil, cover with a lid and gently boil for about 35 minutes or until the rice is tender and the water has been absorbed. Turn off the heat, remove the lid and cover the pan with a folded tea towel. Leave to stand for 10 minutes before fluffing with a fork.

COOKING RED RICE

150g uncooked rice will make approx. 2 servings

Rinse 150g red rice and transfer to a bowl. Cover with cold water and leave to soak for 1–2 hours. Rinse, drain and transfer the rice to a pan with 550ml of cold water. Cover with a lid and bring slowly to the boil, then remove the lid and boil gently over a medium heat until the rice is cooked – about 25–30 minutes or until the grains are tender. Add extra boiling water if needed. Drain off any excess water, then cover the pan with a tea towel. Leave to stand for 5 minutes before fluffing with a fork.

SCENTED RICE

You can add a whole host of ingredients to subtly flavour rice. Simply chop or bruise 3–4 slices of fresh ginger, a lemongrass stalk, star anise or some kaffir lime leaves and add to the rice when cooking. Make sure the flavouring ingredients are large enough to remove easily before serving.

DASHI STOCK

I'm pretty confident that every Japanese household out there always has a supply of dashi to hand. It's the key addition to hundreds of favourite recipes and is also eaten as a soup, on its own or with the addition of other ingredients. It is a stock made from konbu (kelp seaweed), and bonito (dried fish flakes). As with most things, there is always a packet version which you can turn to, but I urge you to make your own as it is so much healthier.

One of the most popular uses for dashi is in the hundreds of Japanese hot pot recipes. Guests dip a variety of foods, from fish to vegetables, in a bubbling table-top cauldron of dashi – rather like a healthy eaters' fondue! The cooked foods are then dipped in tasty sauces and eaten.

Makes approx 800ml

PER 100ML: 7 cals | 0g fat | 0g sat fat | 0.1g protein | 0g carbs 0g sugar | 0.1g salt

15g konbu
15g bonito flakes

Put the konbu into a pan with 1 litre of cold water and leave for about 45 minutes.

Very slowly bring the water to the boil. When it is just about to boil, remove the konbu and discard. Turn up the heat, sprinkle in the bonito flakes and simmer for 15 seconds. Turn off the heat and let the bonito gradually sink to the bottom of the pan. Strain the stock through a very fine-mesh sieve or one lined with muslin and discard the bonito flakes. Pour the dashi into a container and leave to cool.

Keep in the fridge for 3–4 days or the freezer for 3–4 weeks.

COCONUT DRESSING

The Chicken, Prawn & Pomelo Salad (see page 64) uses this dressing. But it would be equally delicious with a chicken or duck salad, or a crab and avocado salad.

Enough for 4–6 servings of salad

PER PORTION (FOR 6): 22 cals | 1.5g fat | 0.6g sat fat | 0.5g protein 1.7g carbs | 1.4g sugar | 0.7g salt

1–1/12 tablespoons Thai Red Curry Paste (see page 174)
4 tablespoons light coconut milk
1 tablespoon fish sauce
1 teaspoon palm sugar or clear honey, preferably raw
4–6 tablespoons lime juice

In a small non-stick pan dry-fry the Thai paste for 2 minutes. Remove from the heat and whisk in the remaining ingredients, adding the lime juice to taste. Transfer to a jug and set aside to cool.

LEMONGRASS AND LIME DRESSING

A versatile, healthier syrup that will transform a platter of sliced fruits such as mango, papaya, longan, lychee, pineapple or strawberries into something special.

Enough for 6–8 servings of fruit salad

PER SERVING (FOR 8): 28 cals | 0g fat | 0g sat fat | 0g protein 7g carbs | 7g sugar | 0g salt

juice of 1/2 large orange
bunch of mint
50g palm sugar
zest and juice of 2 unwaxed limes
1 lemongrass stalk, cut into 4–5 pieces

Pour the orange juice into a small pan with 100ml cold water, the stalks from the mint, the sugar, lime zest and lemongrass. Bring up to a simmer and bubble gently for about 5 minutes or until the liquid has reduced to about 100ml.

Strain through a fine-mesh sieve into a jug, discard the stalks etc and squeeze the juice from 1 of the limes. Taste and adjust, if required – the dressing should be sweet but sharp. Set aside to cool. When cool, pour over sliced fruit and scatter with the mint.

ORANGE & SESAME DRESSING

Use this light and zingy dressing on mixed leaves or with the Rainbow Slaw on page 58 instead of the peanut dressing.

Enough for 6 servings of salad

PER TABLESPOON: 28 cals | 2.5g fat | 0.4g sat fat | 0g protein 1g carbs | 1g sugar | 0.1g salt

juice of 1/2 orange
1 tablespoon red wine or rice vinegar
3cm piece of fresh ginger, peeled and grated
1 teaspoon sesame oil
1/2 heaped teaspoon Dijon mustard
1 1/2 tablespoons light olive oil
2 teaspoons toasted sesame seeds
10–15 small mint leaves
salt and freshly ground black pepper

Put all the ingredients in a screw-top lidded jar and shake well. Taste, adding extra tartness (orange or vinegar), seasoning or oil as required.

PEANUT DRESSING

A great salad dressing for a rice noodle salad, a chicken or prawn and crunchy veg salad or the Rainbow Slaw on page 58.

Enough for 6–8 servings of salad

PER SERVING (FOR 8): 62 cals | 6g fat | 0.6g sat fat | 1g protein 1.5g carbs | 1g sugar | 0.3g salt

1 teaspoon clear honey, preferably raw
3 tablespoons light olive oil
2 teaspoons crunchy peanut butter
1 tablespoon chopped roasted peanuts
1 garlic clove, crushed
1 heaped teaspoon grated fresh ginger
2 teaspoons reduced-salt soy sauce
2 tablespoons rice vinegar
generous squeeze of lime
1 tablespoon hot water
salt and freshly ground black pepper

Put all the ingredients into a bowl, season and whisk until combined. Taste, adding extra vinegar, peanut butter or oil as required. Transfer to a jug to serve.

THAI RED CURRY PASTE

I am a huge fan of the late Keith Floyd, who looked after my friend Suzanne and I when we were travelling and cooking around Ireland. We met Keith in a pub we were cooking for in Kinsale and when he heard we were camping, he very kindly offered for us to stay with him. He was quite the gentleman, cooked us a magnificent roast lamb and charged us £10 a week for cornflakes and loo roll! His Thai red curry paste has always been a favourite, adapted and fiddled with over time, and this version doesn't contain a madly long list of ingredients. If you have the time, I would recommend making your own rather than resorting to shop-bought. Not only is it far tastier but more importantly you know exactly what's in it. The recipe does contain a small amount of salt, but if you want to leave it out, then do – just add a bit more fish sauce when seasoning. Also, if you're a serious chilli fan but can't find the bird's eye ones, I recommend throwing in a 1/2 teaspoon or so of dried chilli flakes.

Makes enough for approximately 3-4 curries, serving 4 people (approx. 12 tablespoons)

(L-GI) (GF) (DF) (LS) (LF)
PER CURRY (SERVES 4): 118 cals | 11.5g fat | 9.5g sat fat | 1.5g protein 3g carbs | 2g sugar 0.7g salt

4 large red chillies, 2 deseeded, all chopped
3 bird's eye chillies, with seeds, chopped
5 garlic cloves
1 small red onion or 2 red shallots, chopped
1 lemongrass stalk, tough outer leaves removed and remaining inner stalk very finely chopped
5 fresh or 8 dried kaffir lime leaves, finely shredded, or the zest of 2 unwaxed limes
1 tablespoon grated fresh ginger or galangal
1 teaspoon coriander seeds, ground, or 1/2 teaspoon ground coriander
1/2 teaspoon cumin seeds, ground, or 1/2 teaspoon ground cumin
5 cloves, ground, or 1/2 teaspoon ground cloves
3 tablespoons chopped coriander stems and roots
1 teaspoon dried shrimp paste, or 3 canned anchovies, drained
1/2 heaped teaspoon sea salt
4 tablespoons coconut or light olive oil
10 white or 6 black peppercorns, crushed

Put all the ingredients into a processor and whizz until the mixture resembles a paste. A smaller processor works best, but you can use a bigger one – just keep scraping down the sides. Alternatively, use a large pestle and mortar. Transfer the paste to an airtight lidded container and keep in the fridge for up to 2-3 weeks or freeze in ice-cube trays, ready to use as needed.

BURMESE CURRY PASTE

This Burmese curry paste is totally different to Vietnamese/Thai-style pastes as it is a largely onion- and garlic-based curry paste that consists of few ingredients and is more spice-led than chilli-based, using hot paprika to add heat. I highly recommend you make a large quantity as below and freeze it in portions to pull out for easy midweek suppers.

Makes enough for approximately 2 curries, each serving 4-6

(L-GI) (GF) (DF) (LS) (LF)

Per portion (serves 4): 74 cals | 4.5g fat | 3.5g sat fat 2g protein | 7g carbs | 4g sugar | 0.2g salt

4 medium onions, quartered
15 garlic cloves
10cm piece of fresh ginger, peeled and sliced
1 teaspoon cayenne pepper
2 teaspoons hot paprika
2 tablespoons coconut or light olive oil
1 teaspoon dried shrimp paste or 3 canned anchovies, drained (optional)
1 teaspoon sea salt
freshly ground black pepper

In a blender combine all the ingredients with 150ml of cold water and a good grinding of black pepper. Blend until it resembles a paste.

Scrape the paste into a medium heavy-based pan and cook over a low to medium heat for 15–20 minutes or until it turns a slightly richer colour and thickens. Stir the paste as it cooks to avoid it catching on the bottom of the pan. Transfer to an airtight container and keep in the fridge for up to 2 weeks, or alternatively freeze for later use.

LAKSA PASTE

This is not only delicious for East meets West Laksa – a noodle-based coconut soup on page 114, but also as a curry paste to use with chicken. Simply fry some cubed chicken and paste, then throw in some coconut milk and simmer. Add a squeeze of lime, some fish sauce to taste and a handful of coriander before serving with rice.

Makes enough for approximately 3 curries, each serving 4

(V) (VE) (L-GI) (DF) (LS)

Per tablespoon: 45 cals | 4g fat | 1g sat fat | 0.7g protein 1.5g carbs | 0.8g sugar

4 long red chillies, with seeds, roughly sliced
3 lemongrass stalks, tough outer leaves removed and remaining inner stalks very finely chopped
12.5cm piece of fresh galangal or ginger, peeled and sliced
6 garlic cloves, halved
5–10 shallots (about 100g), roughly chopped
1 tablespoon coconut or light olive oil
50g macadamia or cashew nuts

Put all the ingredients, apart from the nuts, into a food processor and blitz or pound using a pestle and mortar, until the mixture resembles a rough paste. Add the nuts and pulse or pound until roughly chopped – about 4 quick pulses should do it. Transfer to a container and keep in the fridge until ready to use. It will keep for up to 2 weeks.

VIETNAMESE FRAGRANT GREEN CURRY PASTE

A versatile paste that is mild, zesty and fragrant and can be used for fish, prawns, beef or vegetables as well as the Vietnamese Fragrant Green Chicken Curry on page 119. It contains lots of healing turmeric as well as a wealth of good-for-you aromatics and spices. This freezes brilliantly or will keep for up to 2 weeks in the fridge. Use 3 chillies for a medium strength paste or 5 for a fiery paste. If you want a super-strength paste, throw in some bird's eye chillies too!

Makes enough for approximately 2 curries, each serving 3–4

(V) (VE) (LG) (DF) (LS) (LF)
PER SERVING (FOR 1 CURRY SERVING 4): 23 cals | 1.5g fat 1g sat fat | 0.5g protein | 2g carbs 2g sugar | trace salt

2 lemongrass stalks, tough outer leaves removed and remaining inner stalks very finely chopped

3 large garlic cloves, roughly chopped

3 large green chillies, with seeds, roughly chopped

2 tablespoons roughly chopped coriander stems and roots

4 fresh or 6 dried kaffir lime leaves, shredded

6–8cm piece of fresh ginger, peeled and roughly chopped

zest of 1 large unwaxed lime

2 teaspoons ground turmeric

1 teaspoon curry powder

1 tablespoon coconut or light olive oil

4 teaspoona tamarind purée (see page 92, optional)

2 heaped teaspoons green or pink peppercorns in brine, rinsed and drained

Put all the ingredients, except the peppercorns, along with 2 tablespoons of cold water into a mini processor and blend for 30 seconds or until the mixture resembles a coarse paste. Stir in the peppercorns. Transfer the paste into airtight containers and chill in the fridge for up to 2 weeks or freeze, ready to use as needed.

MASSAMAN CURRY PASTE

A well-known Thai paste that packs just enough punch for the curry lover. Use with chicken, beef or veggie curries, or for the Massaman Chicken Tray Bake on page 120.

Makes enough for approximately 2 curries, each serving 6

(LG) (DF) (LS)
PER SERVING (FOR 1 CURRY SERVING 6): 2 cals | 0g fat | 0g sat fat 0g protein | 0.5g carbs | 0.2g sugar | trace salt

10 dried long red chillies

50g shallots

2 lemongrass stalks, tough outer leaves removed and remaining inner stalks very finely chopped

1 teaspoon shrimp paste

2 teaspoons ground coriander

1 teaspoon ground cumin

¾ teaspoon ground cinnamon

¼ teaspoon ground cloves

½ teaspoon ground white pepper

3 garlic cloves, chopped

3cm piece of fresh galangal or ginger, peeled and chopped

Boil the kettle. Soak the chillies in boiling water for 10 minutes, then drain, reserving the liquid. Deseed the chillies and roughly chop.

Put into a small processor with the remaining ingredients and blitz to a paste, adding enough of the soaking water to form a thickish, rough paste. Transfer the paste to an airtight container and chill in the fridge for up to 2 weeks, ready to use as needed.

PICKLED VEGETABLES

A combination of colourful crunchy vegetables coated in a palette cleansing mix of spices and a sweet sour sauce is a wonderful side dish to serve with some of the richer curries in the book, like the beef rendang or with cold roast meats such as leftover Christmas ham. It will last for a few weeks in a clean jar in the fridge. Ideally try to find a mango that is just starting to give a little when squeezed. Hopefully then you will have a mix of chunks and some slightly more mushy mango, which adds natural sweetness.

Makes 6 servings

(V)(L-3)(GF)(DF)(LS)(LF)

Per serving: 67 cals | 0.5g fat | 2g protein
13g carbs | 13g sugar | 0g salt

200g cauliflower, cut into small florets

1 medium carrot, peeled, cut into 1cm slices on the diagonal and each piece cut in half

1 teaspoon brown mustard seeds

6 cardamon pods, bashed

1 cinnamon stick

1 large red or green chilli, split through nearly the whole way

1 teaspoon ground turmeric

2 ½ tablespoons clear honey, preferably raw

100ml cider vinegar

1 slightly under ripe small mango, cut into 1cm wide x 5cm long strips

1 Japanese cucumber or ½ English cucumber, peeled, halved, deseeded and cut into 1 cm thick slices

Bring a pan of generously salted water to the boil, add the cauliflower and carrots, put on a lid and cook for 2½ minutes exactly, then drain. Add the mustard seeds, cardamon, cinnamon stick, chilli, turmeric, honey, vinegar and 100ml water to the pan and very gently simmer for about 10 minutes.

Check for sweetness and sourness, adjusting to taste by adding extra vinegar or honey, then add the raw and blanched vegetables and mango and stir over the heat giving a good coating of pickling liquid. Cover with a lid and simmer for a further 5-7 minutes, stirring two or three times. The cauliflower, cucumber and carrot should still be nice and crunchy but some of the mango should have formed a lovely syrupy sauce.

Pour straight into a warm sterilized jar, unless you are planning to eat it all straight away, in which case pour into a bowl and once cool, keep in the fridge.

Tip: To sterilise jars, wash the jars and lids in hot soapy water and transfer the jars, but not the lids, to a preheated oven at 150°C/gas mark 2 for 5 minutes.

NUOC CHAM SWEET CHILLI & LIME DIPPING SAUCE

Probably the most popular dipping sauce in Vietnam used for everything from fishcakes to spring rolls. The great thing about it is that it's super quick to make and very low in fat. It is used in the recipe for Prawn & Lemongrass Pops (see page 19), Vietnamese Summer Rolls (see page 35) and Pork Patties (see page 150).

Makes enough sauce for 15-20 nibbles

(LGi)(GF)(DF)(LS)(LF)
PER TEASPOON: 5 cals | 0g fat | 0g sat fat | 0g protein | 0.8g carbs 0.8g sugar | 0.15g salt

1 large red chilli, roughly chopped (deseed for less heat)
1 garlic clove
juice of 1 lime
1 tablespoon fish sauce
1½ tablespoons rice vinegar
2–3 teaspoons clear honey, preferably raw, or a sprinkling of stevia, to taste

Pound the chilli and garlic together using a pestle and mortar to release their juices, then mix together with all the remaining ingredients, plus 2 tablespoons of cold water. Transfer to a small bowl, to serve, or store in an airtight container in the fridge for up to a week.

PLUM SAUCE

Buying sweet, ripe plums for this recipe is the best way of keeping it healthy as you won't need to add so much sugar to sweeten the sauce. This is really like a puréed chutney and is incredibly versatile – a little goes a long way.

From Five Spice Roast Duck on page 137 to the Fresh Duck, Spring Onion & Hoisin Rolls on page 32 it is a much fresher alternative to the high-salt and high-sugar shop-bought plum sauce. You can also smear it over Cheddar and crusty bread or use it to marinate pork fillet before roasting.

Makes 700ml

(V)(LGi)(DF)(LF)
PER 25ML: 19 cals | 0g fat | 0g sat fat | 0.4g protein | 4g carbs 4g sugar

1 cinnamon stick
3 star anise
1 medium red onion, chopped
5 garlic cloves, thinly sliced
3cm piece of fresh ginger, peeled and chopped
1 long red chilli, trimmed and split in 2
1kg sweet, ripe red plums, stoned and quartered
3 tablespoons reduced-salt soy sauce
100ml rice wine vinegar
2–3 tablespoons clear honey, preferably raw

Put all the ingredients, except the honey, into a medium pan and pour in 100ml of cold water. Bring to the boil and then simmer for 45 minutes.

Remove the pan from the heat and strain the contents through a coarse sieve or fine colander, pressing through with the back of a wooden spoon. Reheat the sauce in a clean pan, adding 2 tablespoons of the honey, and bubble for 5 minutes, stirring all the time. The sauce should be a runny ketchup consistency. Taste for sweetness, adding a little more honey if required. Set aside to cool.

Pour into freezerproof lidded containers and store in the freezer or transfer to sterilised jars and screw the lids on whilst the sauce is still warm and keep in the fridge for a few weeks, if unopened.

TERIYAKI SAUCE

Shop-bought teriyaki sauce can contain high amounts of salt and sugar, so is best avoided – especially as the homemade version with ginger and garlic is really tasty and takes minutes to prepare. This is particularly good with beef, chicken, salmon and whole quail.

Makes enough to marinade meat or poultry for 4–6

(V) (L-G) (GF) (DF) (LS) (LF)

Per serving (for 6): 27 cals | 0.5g fat | 0.1g sat fat | 0.4g protein 5g carbs 3.5g sugar | 0.6g salt

2 teaspoons grated fresh ginger
2 garlic cloves, finely chopped
1 ½ tablespoons clear honey, preferably raw
1 teaspoon sesame oil
2 tablespoons tamari or reduced-salt soy sauce
1 ½ tablespoons mirin

Put all the ingredients into a lidded jar, screw the lid on tightly and shake well until combined. Store in the fridge. Use as a marinade on meat, fish, game or poultry prior to cooking. This is best eaten fresh, but keeps it in the fridge for up to a week.

BASIC SAMBAL

A sambal is a chilli-based paste that can be spooned on top of or stirred into noodles, omelettes and anything else that you want to add a kick to. A little dish of sambal is always a fun addition to a platter of starters, as there are often one or two guests who like to add a bit more of a hit of spice. I have made a versatile basic sambal here, using easy-to-find ingredients but cooked rather than raw, as I think cooking adds a bit more depth to it. You can then add to it if you like. Options include tamarind, shredded coconut, lemongrass, fresh chilli or a whole variety of wonderful fresh herbs too. It's a great thing to have in the fridge as it can be added to a stir-fry or tomato pasta sauce.

Makes approximately 15 teaspoons

(L-G) (DF) (LS)

Per teaspoon: 24 cals | 2g fat | 2g sat fat | 0.1g protein | 1g carbs 0.8g sugar | 0.14g salt

3 tablespoons coconut or light olive oil
4 long red chillies, trimmed and chopped into
  2 cm pieces
3 small shallots, sliced
2 dried chillies, cut in half
5cm piece ginger, peeled and grated
2 garlic cloves, thickly sliced
½ heaped teaspoon palm sugar or honey,
  preferably raw
1 ½ tablespoons lime juice
2 teaspoons fish sauce

Heat the oil and add the fresh chillies and shallots. Sauté gently for 3–4 minutes, then tip in the dried chillies, ginger and garlic and cook for a further 2–3 minutes. Tip into a mini processor or mortar. Add the sugar, lime juice, fish sauce and 2 tablespoons of cold water and pulse or grind until the mixture forms a spoonable paste/sauce (it shouldn't be smooth, but it should be an even paste.) Taste, adding more of anything you think it needs – these types of recipes are meant to be tweaked to suit your taste. Transfer to a serving bowl or store in the fridge until required.

KIMCHI

Kimchi is a Korean recipe of fermented cabbage – a little like sauerkraut, but with a punchy kick of spice. It contains vitamins A, B and C as well as lots of good bacteria and is currently hitting the world as the latest superfood.
A bowlful is a great addition to barbecued meats, rice dishes and to serve alongside curries and stews. Most recipes contain gochugaru, or Korean red pepper flakes, but as it can be hard to find (look online), I have opted for sriracha chilli sauce instead, which is more readily available. If you don't have a tiny processor, then make a double quantity so that you don't struggle to make it into a paste. Kimchi makes a great present too!

Makes 2 x 500g jars

(LG) (GF) (DF) (LS) (LF)

PER 25G SERVING: 7 cals | 0g fat | 0g sat fat | 0.3g protein
1.5g carbs | 1.2g sugar | 1.3g salt

1 head of Chinese cabbage (about 650g), 2 leaves
   kept whole and the remainder shredded into
   5 x 2cm pieces
3 heaped tablespoons flaky sea salt
2 fat garlic cloves, crushed
2 teaspoons grated fresh ginger
2 teaspoons sriracha sauce, or more for extra
   fiery flavour
2 teaspoons clear honey, preferably raw
1 eating apple, peeled, cored and sliced
2 tablespoons fish sauce
4 spring onions, trimmed and cut into 2cm pieces
1 large carrot, cut into 2 mm slices

Place the shredded cabbage in a large colander over a bowl and sprinkle with the salt. Toss to combine. Cover and set aside for about 1 1/2 hours to wilt and release some juice.

Meanwhile, put the garlic, ginger, sriracha sauce, honey, apple and fish sauce in a mini food processor with 7 tablespoons of cold water. Process the mixture until it forms a rough paste, scraping the sides as needed.

Once the cabbage has wilted, thoroughly rinse off the salt under cold running water and drain well in a colander over a large bowl, weighed down with a plate for 1-2 hours.

Add the cabbage to the bowl, with the paste, spring onions and carrots. Mix thoroughly.

To sterilise the jars, wash 2 x 500g jars and lids in hot soapy water and transfer just the jars to a preheated oven at 150°C/gas mark 2 for 5 minutes.

Pack the kimchi into the sterilised and still warm jars, making sure that each jar has 3cm of space at the top (if needed, add a further tablespoon or two of water to the jar to make sure the kimchi is just covered by liquid.). Press the mixture down firmly using the wooden spoon, so that the brine covers the top.

Cover the top of each jar with one of the reserved cabbage leaves. Seal the jars loosely, then leave the kimchi to rest for 3 days at room temperature. When the kimchi is ready, seal the jars by screwing the lid on and keep in the fridge for a few weeks.

HEALTHY ASIAN STORECUPBOARD

Beansprouts are widely used in Asian cooking. These crunchy, long, white-fleshed sprouts have a mild, very slightly bitter taste. Ideal in stir-fries, salads and spring rolls, they are added at the last minute to keep their crunch. They are low in calories and rich in vitamins B and C.

Bonito flakes are also known as katsuobushi and are flakes of dried, smoked bonito fish, which is a type of tuna. They are similar in look and texture to wood shavings, with a smoky, fishy taste, and are used to flavour Japanese broths, such as dashi and miso.

Chilli peppers come in many forms and vary in size, shape and colour. Strength also varies greatly from mild to extremely hot. As a general rule, the smaller the chilli, the hotter. The spiciest part of the chilli is found in the interior tissues to which the seeds are attached. Fresh chillies can be chopped and added directly to pastes, curries and stir-fries, whilst dried chillies are ideal for crushing into a powder. Make sure to wear rubber gloves or rub your fingers in salt before handling chillies. Fresh chillies are highly nutritious and are a rich source of vitamin C and antioxidants.

Chilli sauce (sweet) is a storecupboard standby for adding to sauces and stir-fries or for use as a dipping sauce. Watch out though as it can be high in salt and refined sugar, and depending on the brand, can contain preservatives. Fiery yet sweet and syrupy, buy a good-quality brand and check the ingredients list. Better still, make your own or just add some chilli and honey to your dish.

Chinese cabbage is also known as nappa cabbage. It is light in colour, larger than regular cabbage and oblong in shape. It has a mild, sweet, peppery flavour and can be eaten raw in salads or stir-fried. Packed with antioxidants and vitamins C and K, it is also very low in calories.

Chives are long, thin, tubular leaves with purple flowers (English) or white flowers (Chinese). The taste is similar to onion but fresher, lighter and sweeter. Chives are best eaten raw. Part of the allium family, chives have been studied in relation to their cancer-preventing organosulfur compounds. They are a good source of allicin, which is said to lower both cholesterol and blood pressure.

Coconut milk/cream Coconut milk is a creamy white liquid taken from the flesh of coconuts. It is the main ingredient in most south-east Asian curries. Like dairy cream, coconut cream floats to the top, whereas the milk is the thinner, more watery liquid below. Light/low-fat coconut milk is coconut milk that is either diluted with water or is the thinner milk from the pressed coconut. Creamed coconut and coconut milk are made in a way surprisingly akin to their dairy counterparts: coconut flesh (the white part) is grated and soaked in hot water; the coconut cream then rises to the top and can be skimmed off; the remaining liquid is squeezed through a cheesecloth to extract a white liquid that is coconut milk. By repeating this process, the coconut milk becomes thinner. Thin coconut milk is used for cooking curries and soups, whereas the thicker version is used for desserts and rich sauces.

Coconut oil is a very healthy choice for cooking. Although it is high in saturated fat (so use in moderation), it contains medium-chain triglycerides, which can be absorbed into the body without the digestion normally required for fat. It also doesn't seem to have the same effect on blood cholesterol as other fats. It can be used in high-heat cooking as well as in dressings. Despite its slightly sweet coconut aroma, it is ideal for savoury cooking. It is more expensive than most other oils but well worth the price tag. Hugely popular due to its health benefits (including being rich in lauric acid), it can help kill bacteria.

Coconut water is the liquid held inside a young coconut. It has a subtle, slightly sweet taste. Make sure to buy the pure, unsweetened version. Packed with simple sugars, electrolytes and minerals, it is a great energy drink for rehydrating the body (and ideal for diarrhoea sufferers). It is said to have a host of health and beauty benefits, including antiaging properties, and aiding problems with digestion and metabolism.

Coriander is also known as cilantro or Chinese parley. The entire plant is edible: the small, round, yellow-brown seeds can be used whole or ground; the leaves have a light, fresh flavour tinged with lemon and are often eaten raw and added to dishes at the very end; and the stems are cooked in sauces, soups and curries and have a slightly milder taste than the leaves. Coriander seeds have a health-supporting reputation that is high on the list of healing spices. Coriander has also been referred to as an anti-diabetic plant. It is also known for its anti-inflammatory properties, as well as for its cholesterol-lowering effects.

Curry paste – I recommend you make your own curry paste as it will taste so much nicer made with fresh ingredients and it also freezes well. If you do opt for ready-made, buy a good-quality brand and check the ingredients.

Daikon is a large, white Asian radish with a light peppery taste similar to watercress. High in antioxidants and vitamin C, it also aids digestion and weight loss.

Dried shrimp are shrimp that have been sundried and shrunk to thumbnail size. They have a fishy, savoury (umami) taste and are a great addition to curry pastes and salads. Often used in Chinese medicine, dried shrimp are rich in calcium and magnesium, which can help heart function and reduce cholesterol.

Fish sauce is made from fermented fish and sea salt. It is an amber-coloured liquid that is used to add a salty flavour to dishes. Use sparingly to avoid sending the salt content of your dish soaring. It has a distinctly salty, fishy taste. It is high in protein, vitamins and minerals.

Five spice powder is a blend of spices that usually includes fennel seeds, cinnamon, cloves, star anise and peppercorns. Highly aromatic, the combination encompasses five flavours: sweet, sour, salty, spicy and pungent. All the spices have different benefits, including easing stomach aches, inflammation and dizziness.

Galangal is an Asian plant that is part of the ginger family. As such, it is similar to ginger but has a more potent, fiery flavour. As it is very hard in texture, it requires a sharp knife or grater to cut it. If you can't get hold of it, substitute with fresh ginger. As it contains anti-inflammatory properties, it is beneficial in the treatment of arthritis. Like ginger, it can help relieve abdominal discomfort and nausea. It also contains a host of antioxidants.

Ginger – Young ginger can be eaten raw, pickled or used to make tea – it is juicier and milder than mature ginger, which is more potent and is used to flavour dishes. It is promoted by some as a cancer treatment as it can apparently slow down or prevent tumour growth. It also relieves abdominal discomfort and nausea, and is an anti-inflammatory, helping with arthritis pain. It also contains a host of antioxidants.
Pickled ginger is sweet, slightly hot, thinly sliced young ginger that has been marinated in sugar and vinegar. It is usually eaten with sushi or sashimi (raw fish). Ginger has antiseptic properties and was originally eaten with sushi to counter the effects of bad fish.

Hoisin sauce is a sweet, spicy, dark red sauce made from soya beans, vinegar, sugar, garlic and various spices. Thankfully, a little goes a long way as it is high in salt and sugar. Always buy good-quality hoisin to avoid ingredients lists that are full of additives and preservatives.

Honey is a natural, tasty sweetener that works in sweet and savoury dishes. Whilst it does have high fructose levels, it contains a bounty of cancer-defending antioxidants. Try and use raw honey as it contains far more nutrients.

Kaffir lime leaves are aromatic green leaves from the kaffir lime plant – not to be mistaken for the lime tree. Kaffir lime fruits are not usually eaten (they are widely used for their zest oil) as they are very bitter, but the leaves have a more subtle, aromatic, slightly bitter fragrance. They are

used mainly in Thai cooking to add a zesty but aromatic flavour to curries and soups. If you can find fresh, then buy a bunch and store them in a plastic food bag in the freezer. Otherwise use dried and double the quantity.

Kai lan is also known as Chinese broccoli or Chinese kale. It is a leaf vegetable that has thick, flat, glossy, blue-green leaves with thick stems and a small number of tiny flower heads. It is similar in taste to broccoli but slightly more bitter. It is a nutrient-dense food that provides an excellent source of vitamins A, C and K, as well as a great source of folic acid, and has a high amount of dietary fibre.

Lemongrass is a fragrant tropical grass and an Asian storecupboard essential. It is best used either finely chopped/ground in pastes or in large pieces that can be removed in curries and soups, as well as tea. The oil yielded from bashing the stems gives a lemony fragrance. Citral, the chemical found in lemongrass, has many benefits, including positive effective on the body's ability to use vitamin A. Lemongrass also has rubefacient properties, meaning that it may be able to improve blood circulation.

Mango is a fleshy, oval, yellow-red tropical fruit that is eaten ripe or used green in pickles and salads. The fruit has a sweet, fragrant flesh with a mild tartness. It is rich in pre-biotic dietary fibre, vitamins, minerals and antioxidants, which amongst other things help protect against many kinds of cancer and help lower blood pressure.

Mint is a wonderfully refreshing addition to many Asian recipes. It goes well with both coriander and Thai basil. Mint is soft but quite pungent and a little goes a long way. Buy fresh-looking green mint, ideally as a bunch. Keep it in the fridge wrapped in damp kitchen paper. Add to dishes at the end of cooking or just before serving.

Mirin is a rice wine used for flavouring Japanese dishes. It has a strong, sweet, slightly vinegary wine flavour and is used as a sweetener in stir-fries, sauces and marinades.

Miso paste is a savoury Japanese paste made principally from fermented soya beans. It is typically salty, but different varieties of miso have been described as salty, sweet, earthy, fruity and savoury. Though miso is very high in salt, it does have some health benefits due to the presence of lecithin, which is effective in the prevention of high blood pressure.

Oyster sauce is a condiment traditionally made from simmering down oysters in water until caramelised. This rich, sweet and salty sauce is used to give flavour to a base sauce. However, it's important to buy good-quality brands as many use short cuts and contain MSG.

Pak choi is a leafy green Chinese vegetable similar to

spinach, which has long, green, slightly ribbed leaf stalks and soft oval green leaves. The leaves taste a little like spinach and the white stalks (which stay crunchy even after stir-frying) have a subtle, slightly nutty flavour. It is better cooked (stir-fried or in soups), than eaten raw and is a very rich source of many vital phytonutrients, vitamins, minerals and health-benefiting antioxidants.

Palm sugar is a crystalline sweetener that looks, tastes, dissolves and melts almost exactly like sugar but is completely natural. It is made by boiling the nectar of the coconut palm in a two-stage process, which leaves a hard, caramel-type substance. With a delicious caramel/ butterscotch flavour, it is a perfect sugar to use in some, but not all, recipes. It often comes packed in a pot as a very firm but just-spoonable block. It can also be even firmer and requires cutting and then grating. However, it is now available in some supermarkets in a large granular form and as a powder. It is widely used in Asian dressings to counteract saltiness and is often added to curries for a subtle sweetness. Add to puddings, too, for a smooth buttery taste and texture. Low in GI, it is naturally rich in a number of key vitamins, minerals and phytonutrients, including potassium, zinc, iron and B vitamins.

Panko is the Japanese word for 'breadcrumbs' and is a crispy coating or topping used instead of regular breadcrumbs. The white flakes are made without using crusts from the whole loaf. They are much flakier than regular breadcrumbs and the oil doesn't soak into them so much, resulting in more crunch and a lighter texture.

Pomelo is similar in taste and texture to grapefruit, but the flesh is slightly more sweet than sour. Rich in vitamins A, B and C, it also contains high amounts of betacarotene and folic acid. It also contains a good amount of potassium, which keeps the heart healthy, as well as bioflavonoids, healthy fats, protein, fibre, antioxidants and enzymes.

Rice vinegar is made from fermented rice or rice wine.

Sake is sometimes referred to as rice wine. Japanese sake is made primarily from rice and is brewed using a micro-organism called koji and then fermented. It is brewed using a process more similar to beer-making than wine-making. Sake is mildly more alcoholic than wine, with an alcohol content ranging from 13-16 per cent. It varies in type by how polished the rice is: daiginjo is the top designation, with at least 50 per cent of the rice milled; ginjo has 40 per cent; and honjozo has 30 per cent milled. It is a wonderful addition to many Asian dishes and is gaining popularity for use in western dishes too. It is clean and dry tasting. Used rather like Shaoxing or white wine in cooking, it is available from most supermarkets.

Sesame oil is great for adding flavour to dressings and has a delicate nutty taste of toasted sesame seeds. It has a high smoking point so is good for stir-frying. It is extremely nutritious and an excellent source of copper, calcium, magnesium and iron.

Sesame seeds (white and black) have a delicate nutty taste and add a lovely subtle crunch to dishes, especially when toasted. They are available in a variety of colours including brown, red, black, yellow and ivory. The darker seeds are said to have the most flavour. Toss into salads or use as a healthy crunchy coating to fish and meat. Sesame paste (tahini) can be used as a peanut butter substitute and makes a great addition to Middle-Eastern dishes. Because it has one of the highest oil contents of any seed, it should be kept in the fridge. Sesame seeds are an excellent source of copper, manganese, calcium, magnesium, iron, phosphorus, vitamin B1 and zinc. They also contain two unique substances: sesamin and sesamolin, both of which have been shown to have a cholesterol-lowering effect.

Shiitake mushrooms are an Asian edible fungus with enormous superfood properties. Not only delicious in stir-fries, immune-boosting mushrooms have been heralded and used in Chinese medicine for hundreds of years. More recently shiitake mushrooms, in particular, have been the focus of wider research into cancer treatment. Studies have found that the lentinan that it contains was showing great cancer-fighting properties as well as helping combat the side effects of cancer treatment.

Snake beans are also known as long beans, yardlong beans, bora, long-podded cowpeas, asparagus beans, pea beans and Chinese long beans. They are dark green, thin and long (up to 90cm when uncurled), with a slightly sweet flavour and crunchy texture. They're ideal chopped in stir-fries and curries or served in Asian side dishes. Look for firm bright green beans with no yellowing. These high-fibre beans are also high in vitamins A and C.

Soy sauce is a condiment made from a fermented paste of boiled soya beans. A traditional ingredient in Asian cooking, it is a salty-tasting liquid used to add a salty–savoury (umami) flavouring to dishes.

Star anise, as the name suggests, is a Chinese spice that resembles a star shape and is closely related to the anise plant. It is one of the spices in Chinese five spice powder. It has a bark-like texture and should be discarded after cooking. The essential oil, anethole, is what gives the spice its liquorice flavour and it is a wonderful addition to stews and soups. Add at the start of cooking to let the flavour infuse over time. There has been research to show that it is a natural fighter against the fungus Candida albicans. It is also said to have antibacterial and antioxidant properties.

Stevia is a powder made from the Stevia plant. It is not an Asian ingredient, but a great alternative to sugar as it is a natural sweetener that has virtually no calories and does not affect blood glucose levels.

Sugar is THE hot topic at the moment and wading through the blurb out there, my general feeling is that although pretty much all sugar is bad for you, I suggest natural un-mucked about with sugar/sweeteners eaten in small quantities. Stevia, raw honey, palm sugar and maple syrup get the highest points as they are relatively easy to find, come from natural sources and at least you know what you are eating (in fact you might even gain some health benefits too). Anything artificial or highly refined definitely doesn't get my vote I'm afraid. Nor am I massively keen to include rice malt syrup or coconut syrup as I think you are entering the rather more niche section of the health food store, which would put me off, if you're not on a fructose free diet, but trying to use an everyday healthy-eating cookbook!

Tamari is thicker, richer and less salty than most soy sauces, and the flavour tends to be smoother. The brown pigment in tamari has strong antioxidant and anti-cancer properties. It is also said to aid the digestion of grains and vegetables whilst being rich in several minerals. It should be gluten-free so can be used as an alternative to soy sauce in any of the recipes, but make sure you use a good-quality brand.

Tamarind has a sour–sweet taste. It comes in the form of a paste in the Asian section of large supermarkets. Specialist Asian supermarkets may sell the pulp form, which needs breaking down with a small amount of boiling water to make a purée so that it can be added to dishes. Tamarind can be taken for constipation, liver and gallbladder problems, as well as stomach disorders. It is also used to treat colds and fever. Women sometimes use tamarind to treat pregnancy-related nausea. It is given to children to treat intestinal worms.

Teriyaki sauce is a Japanese sauce/marinade made from a mixture of soy sauce, sake, ginger and other flavourings. I love it but highly recommend making your own to avoid a high-salt, high-sugar content and a mass of added nasties from shop-bought versions. The dominant flavour is soy, but with subtle notes of ginger, garlic and sweetness. Use as a marinade for virtually any meat, poultry or fish. Especially great when then barbecued. Use sparingly to keep the salt levels acceptable.

Thai basil is a type of sweet basil native to South-East Asia. Slightly more subtle in taste than European basil, it has a sweet liquorice flavour. It is ideal for use in cooking as

it remains stable when heated. It can also be bought in a paste form, which works well in cooking. Add to salads and Vietnamese summer rolls as well as stir-fries. Often used as a medicinal plant, it is high in antioxidants, has antibacterial properties and offers a good dose of vitamins A and K.

Tofu, or bean curd, is coagulated soy milk which is then pressed into soft white blocks. It is a great vegan substitute to meat. The beauty of tofu is that it has no flavour of its own and acts as a brilliant flavour sponge. Available in most supermarkets in both a silken/soft tofu (ideal for soups, marinades, dressings and deserts) and regular tofu, which is more of a solid block (used chopped in curries and stir-fries). Tofu has a low calorie count and relatively large amounts of protein. It is high in iron and, depending on the coagulants used in manufacturing, is often high in calcium and/or magnesium.

Turmeric is a yellow aromatic powdered spice obtained from the rhizome (root stem) of a plant of the ginger family. It is mainly used for flavouring curry. It has an earthy, slightly bitter, slightly hot, peppery flavour and a mustardy smell. Though commonly used in Indian cooking and curries, I recommend that you add it whenever you can, as it is mild enough to go unnoticed but powerful enough to fight health wars all around the globe! Do make sure you buy good-quality turmeric though. It is a total wonder spice that has antiseptic qualities and contains curcumin, which is use to treat cancer, Alzheimer's and diabetes.

Wonton wrappers are made from flour, egg, water and salt, and are used as wrappers for dumplings. They have a pasta-like texture and are usually filled with a meat, fish or veggie mixture and then steamed, boiled, fried or grilled.

Wasabi, or Japanese horseradish, is a hot green paste used to accompany Japanese raw fish (sashimi) and sushi. It has a fiery mustardy flavour similar to horseradish. Mostly used either spread thinly on fish or diluted in a dipping sauce such as soy sauce. Only a small amount is required as it is very strong. Possibly originally used for its antimicrobial properties, hence the pairing with raw fish. Wasabi is also an anti-inflammatory and can promote liver health.

INDEX

ACKNOWLEDGEMENTS

I can't believe we're here again my lovely family and friends! Yet again I couldn't have done it without you. Special thanks to my dear friend (and awesome cook) Charlotte Petch, who has helped me every step of the way, adding so many great ideas and improvements to the book – especially when it came to the suggested addition of weird healthy ingredients! A huge thank-you also to our wonderful helper Helen, who we couldn't do without for about a thousand reasons! To my chief tasters, Andrew, Wilbo and Jemima. Your honesty and enthusiasm always keeps my feet on the ground and a smile on my face! Thanks to 'the team' - nutrition whizz Fiona Hunter, photographer Alicia Taylor, food stylist Deborah Kaloper, home economist Emma Christian, designer Aileen Lord and of course my marvellous book editor Sophie Allen – I'm so pleased you have moved up the road! Thankfully I think we've been pretty in sync on this, and as a result it's been a real pleasure – even if we didn't ever agree on the addition of congee porridge! Kyle, a thousand thank-you's for supporting both me and my ideas. You said about 8 years ago that if I stuck with you, you would nurture me as a writer, and you have kept your word, which I am hugely grateful to you for – especially as I have in the time moved continents! And of course to Judith, Victoria, Hannah and the whole Kyle books team – you are incredibly with it and on it, and for that I thank you!

There are also a worldwide spread of thank-yous to so many good friends who helped test the recipes for the book and gave me loads of great tips and ideas: Sophie Allen, Rachel Baker, Claire Broadley, Fiona Cameron, Lucy Carlbom, Emily Cheetham, Melsie Clegg, Kirsty Cornell, Harry Cox, Jane (Mum) Drysdale, Sophie Edmunds, Clare Evelyn, Sukie Fletcher, Millie Godman, Tula Goodwin, Kate Harris, Caroline Hulbert, Hilary James, Kit and M-J James, Claire Jelf, Linda Kingdon, Tory Lodder, Tania MacCallum, Sophie Martin, Gemma and Jim Moffatt, Becky Menzies, Jodie O Doherty, Edith Pacis, Clare Pannell, Fiona Philip, Karen Pilkington, Sarah Prior, Francesca Rathbone, Lucy Ridgwell, Al Studd, Henry and Livs Syrett, Marcus and Becca Taylor, Kat Thompson, Alex Urquhart, Fiona Vogel, Richard and Belinda Warburton, Dawn Wright, and the person I am guaranteed to have forgotten or spelt their name wrong!

Thanks to all the suppliers who've helped and supported me and those who are so kindly promoting and selling my books. Especially to mention: Meat the Butcher, Fishwives Singapore, Shiva Designs, Spin Singapore, Korla and the smaller suppliers and shops both in Asia and the farthest reaches of Scotland who have been willing to give my books a go.

INDEX